A SUMMER IN '69

Dee Davidson Dosch

Eloquent Books
Durham, Connecticut

Eloquent Books
An imprint of Strategic Book Group
P.O. Box 333
Durham CT 06422
www.StrategicBookGroup.com

ISBN: 978-1-60911-207-3

Photographs prepared by Erik Carlgren

Book Design: Bruce Salender

Printed in the United States of America.

This story is dedicated to my traveling buddies,
Dr. Meri Shadley and Melody Jones Richardson.

ACKNOWLEDGMENTS

Without the encouragement of numerous individuals, from my associates at Suncadia Resorts, work connections in Port Angeles, to my colleagues and acquaintances in Ellensburg, Washington, this book would not have been completed. I would especially like to thank the family of the late Edwin C. Brunton, my good friend from Sequim, who took the time to read my rough draft and made some necessary corrections and suggestions for me to go forward with this publication.

I would also like to mention another special friend from Colorado, Dan Sutherland. He also read an early version and found the story amusing. He encouraged me to write more about the events and history during the sixties and thought the book would be a worthwhile endeavor. I value his thoughts and candor as well as his kindness, honesty, and humor.

My immediate family and close friends were always in my thoughts as I transferred the brief notes in my diary to the extended typed manuscript. The content of this story was made possible through the blessings and support of my mother and father, who allowed the trip to transpire.

Education and travel were valued by my parents. Even as a young girl I was encouraged and expected to pursue my dreams of traveling and visiting other countries. Inspired by pictures in books as well as *National Geographic*, I always knew I would someday have to go to those distant lands. Although we were not a family with great monetary wealth, this was never an obstacle when it came to my interest in seeing new places and living in foreign lands. As the account unfolded, I couldn't help but think about the terrific experience I had with my two girlfriends. These amazing women are exceptionally beautiful, gifted, and accomplished. We have always stayed in contact, and I treasure their friendship to this day.

INTRODUCTION

After living in the Midwest most of my fifty-plus years, I moved to the beautiful northwest state of Washington. My son and his wife lived in the Seattle area, and they were expecting my first grandchild. Despite the fact that I left my friends in Colorado by choice, it was no less difficult making new friends in the town in which I was residing.

After settling in and finding a job, I seemed to have more time on my hands than usual. To help make the depressing, gloomy winter months go by more quickly, I started writing a story about one of the most memorable summers I ever experienced.

In the summer of 1969, I spent three months in Europe with two girlfriends. One of my long-term goals was to write a book about this trip when I had more time. The time had arrived. While unpacking boxes, I came across a diary I kept during that summer. Complete with dates and places, as well as names and addresses of the people I met, it became my main source of reference. I hope my readers find this narrative as entertaining and enjoyable as it was for me.

While reading through the account, I realized this experience influenced many of my adult attitudes. The summer was full of adventure, exploring, surprises, and brief romances. I was able to relive that summer all over again. The names have not been changed to protect anyone. I have not spoken to most of these people in over forty years. My hope is that they don't mind my mentioning their names throughout this memoir.

Keep in mind that this is a true story of three young girls (barely out of their teens) spending the summer in far-away countries. It was the end of a decade when American women were beginning to know and acquire freedoms that were not previously available. The reins were unleashed. Most adolescent girls who grew up in the fifties were either "good girls" or "bad girls." Female roles were restricted and defined. I was a product of my culture at that time and committed to "saving myself for marriage." Having no desire to compromise those moral boundaries, like many girls in the sixties, I just wanted to have fun. So I took advantage of these newfound freedoms.

Not all girls who grew up in the sixties adopted the "free love" mentality. My friends and I were not rebels. We were just longing to enjoy the summer working and traveling in other countries. None of us were street-wise, tough--girl types, but neither were we timid and fragile. However, we were incredibly naive. Adaptability was a trait we possessed and learning to problem-solve, in some awkward and unfamiliar situations, forced solutions as predicaments occurred.

Without being considered a prude, it was still important that I be a virtuous woman. In fact, it was in 1969 that the Catholic Church changed the status of Mary Magdalene, friend of Jesus, from "prostitute" to the faithful follower she always was. Held in fond esteem, she then became a beloved Apostle. It was never mentioned in the Bible that Mary was a sinner prostitute. Most stories only alluded to her "bad girl" image. She is one of my preferred biblical characters.

There were a growing number of women in our country who were outraged with the sexism and the exploitation of females. Economic inequities between men and women were decried by angry feminists. Both rebellious young women and housewives alike were up in arms. My girlfriends and I were neither defiant demonstrators nor protesters. We weren't as interested in changing the world as much as we just wanted to see more of the world. Peacefully.

Race riots, peace rallies, and political protests were occurring in most parts of our country. The majority of the dissent was over concerns and complaints about social justice, civil rights, and the quality of life in America. Not wishing to escape from this turmoil and change, I did yearn for some time away. Writing term papers, and studying and cramming for college exams could be overwhelming. Ready to explore another continent, I was all set to live in a different culture.

I will take you on an extended tour that lasted three months. We worked in several countries with complaints that were justified from our perspective as immature, foreign employees. I am not insinuating that our employers were in any way unjust to Americans. Keeping a daily record in my diary, I noted the places we traveled to and what we saw. The sites I found captivating and interesting may not have been the same for my wanderlust friends. Describing what I recalled to the best of my recollection was not always easy. The journal reminded me of activities and places that were fairly vivid in my mind, but many of the day's events were completely forgotten. Nearly forty years had passed, as well as some memories. We do remember what we want to.

The sixties was a time when it was still relatively safe for girls to hitchhike throughout Europe, without fears of being molested. Computers were rare and cell phones did not even exist. Long distance calls were expensive and infrequent. Making calls to family and friends by telephone was exceedingly impractical. It wasn't even possible to dial up a phone directly overseas without the assistance of an operator. However, limited access to technology, money, and resources did not hinder my motivation or persistence.

Some of my encounters were hilarious and inconceivable. The stories I describe are not made up or exaggerated. We looked forward to every new day in anticipation of what was in store for exploring and seeing. There were a few romantic interludes and always the most extraordinary scenery. Discovering only a fraction of everything there was to see and do, we made our best efforts to cover as much territory as possible. Most days were full of fun and excitement; some days would be stressful and tedious. No day was ever boring. They were the best days of my life!

Forty years later, I sit pecking away at my laptop computer, sharing this incredible story with any interested readers. So sit back, relax, and enjoy this short chronicle of a summer in '69. You will follow the trails of three vivacious, young women as they worked and played in the streets, through the towns, over the mountains, and on the beaches of Western Europe.

CONTENTS

A SUMMER IN '69

While the nation was still divided over the Vietnam conflict, with peace marches and racial protests going on in most of the country, two of my girlfriends and I were preparing to leave on a life-changing journey. For three long months, we intended to work our way through Europe and experience the sights and sounds of foreign travel. I couldn't think of any better way to spend a summer break from studying than to explore my European roots and maybe some European men.

Traveling throughout Europe had been suggested the previous summer while I was working at a mountain lodge in Estes Park, Colorado. My roommate, Nancy Moore, thought it would be fun to work together the following summer and go abroad. Going overseas was a vacation I thought you took after retirement. Returning to our respective colleges, we both completed another year of school.

My parents didn't object to my leaving the country, but our family was not well-off. To make the trip affordable, I secured a part-time evening job while going to classes during the day. Through a student exchange program, Nancy and I were fortunate enough to get positions in Germany. Having jobs waiting with room and board was just the security we needed. I started packing!

1

Since I would be living and working in Germany, I thought it might be a good idea to take Beginning German 101 to get a grasp of the language. Conversational German to order food, shopping, and asking directions were what I needed to learn. I assumed that once I lived in Germany, picking up the language would not be a problem. Nothing could have been further from the truth. Some people have an ear for learning another language. I struggled. Mastering a foreign language was easier said than done. Needless to say, it was not one of my better grades for the semester.

As the spring term came to an end, I couldn't have been more excited. The hectic year with classes, working, and making travel plans were complete. Everything was falling into place and I was anxious to leave. Then I received an unanticipated call from Nancy. She informed me of her engagement. Unfortunately, she would have to cancel her summer plans. Expressing remorse and disappointment, she apologized for the sudden change of heart. Hanging up the telephone in a state of shock, I could hardly believe what I'd heard. After all, the trip was her inspiration. Her marriage to Stan in Wichita, Kansas, went on in spite of me and without my physical presence.

The setback was short lived. Informing a few of my friends about the cancellation of my travel partner, I immediately received an offer from one of my roommates. She would love to go, if she could scrounge up enough cash. Receiving a call from a close childhood friend, she too wanted to go. Having two travel companions could pose a potential problem. There were only two housekeeping jobs.

Although neither of these girls knew each other, they were close friends of mine. How could I pick one over the other to travel with me to Europe? The employment confirmations were in Frankfurt, Germany, at the Steigenberger Airport Hotel. Nonetheless, if they were willing to take a chance that we could get a third offer after arriving in Germany, I would cherish having them travel with me. So, the two-some became a three-some and we made final plans for departure.

Booking the same exact flights was not possible. Icelandic Airlines had the most economical fare. A round-trip ticket cost $369.25, which included a stop overnight in the country of Iceland. Last-minute flight arrangements were finalized; we were determined to make this happen.

Meri Shadley, my Tri-Sigma sorority sister, couldn't get a ticket on the Icelandic flight with the overnighter. Melody Jones, a childhood friend, was able to get a layover flight leaving shortly thereafter. Even with all the finagling, one thing was for sure: I wouldn't be going alone. After required photos were taken, passports ordered, booster shots updated, and the letters of two job appointments, as soon as finals were done, we were headed for an unimaginable passage.

A few months before taking off, I ran into a friend I'd known since junior high school. Mark Beverage was the first boy I ever kissed, on a 4-H hay ride when I was about twelve years old. He was a World War II military buff and especially interested in Nazi Germany relics. While we chatted, I told him of my plans to work in Germany for the summer. He proceeded to inform me that he was going to Germany on a work study. What a coincidence! We just happened to be flying on the exact same flight, leaving from John F. Kennedy Airport, on May the thirtieth. What a twist of fate! Giddily, we continued to discuss securing a ride together to New York City.

On the weekend before I left, my family and friends surprised me with a small going-away party. I went out to dinner with a guy I'd been casually dating. David was a year younger and a friend of one of my brothers. Planning to finish college, I wanted to work a few years before getting involved in a serious relationship. Still, David and I enjoyed each other's company, and we had some really fun times together.

Not suspicious of his taking me out, when we arrived back at my house, several of my closest buddies were there to bid me farewell. The bittersweet gala caused some anxiety and hesitation. I'd planned, saved, organized, and worked for this trip for almost a year. My longing to leave was becoming a reality, but I was having second thoughts. Thinking about the length of time I'd be away from family and friends was distressing. *Will there always be such ambiguity in life?* I wondered.

I posted a "Ride Wanted" note in the student union building at the school that Mark and I attended. Sharing rides with fellow students to help with gas expenses was common practice in those days. Credit cards were not readily available to undergraduates, and none of our parents had money. A student by the name of Dick Wade answered the appeal to leave Springfield, Missouri, on May the twenty-eighth. Dick had a midday final and couldn't get away until the afternoon. Mark and I ate lunch and, eventually, we all headed east to New York on Route 66.

* * *

The heat and humidity of summer surrounded the old, dirty, worn-out car with no airconditioner. Taking turns at the wheel, we drove through the night. Upon reaching the Pennsylvania Turnpike, Dick's car was denied access because of a defective tire. This poor, pathetic guy was not prepared; he had no spare tire or any spare money. Reluctantly, I consented to buying him a used tire for everyone's sake.

In turn, I asked Dick to do me a favor and make a stop on the way so I could visit my little brother. Bill joined the Navy to escape the draft that year, and he was implicated in an automobile accident. While healing from his minor injuries, he was admitted to the United States Naval Hospital in Philadelphia. Dick was more than obliging in honoring my simple request.

Bill was not hurt badly, but the infirmary was full of severely wounded Vietnam War veterans. It broke my heart to see in real life what we'd been hearing about on the news for way too long. My brother walked with me as we visited some of the bed-ridden men who'd lost arms and legs. He pushed the courageous heroes in wheelchairs to their scheduled physical therapy sessions. Seeing what most civilians were denied to see, I realized more than ever that it was past time to end this bloody conflict. Earlier in the month, President Richard Nixon appeared on television to outline an eight-point peace plan. He called for the withdrawal of most U.S. troops within the year.

I kissed Bill good-bye, and we drove on to Douglas, New York. The worst drive of my life was over and Mark and I were elated to be out of that disgusting car. The pleasures and pains of the first leg of the expedition concluded. After making a short phone call, we left Dick behind.

A former Army cohort of my dad lived in Floral Park, New York. I had met him a few years prior when my family took a vacation to the World's Fair. My father made previous arrangements for his friend to pick me up once I arrived on Long Island. Mr. Burke took Mark and me back to a home-cooked meal and a comfy place to spend the night. After the twenty-hour drive, we were exhausted. Their family was more than gracious and I was able to get some much needed sleep.

The following morning, the teenage Burke children, Tricia and Danny, accompanied us to the subway station. Meeting Melody at a Manhattan hotel, she'd flown in the day before from her home in Houston. Several years had passed since we'd seen each other. While walking through Central Park, we were able to catch up on news of family and friends. Hippies, dressed in beaded jeans and gaudy embroidered shirts, were selling their wares spread out on the grass for display. While still in my own homeland, I was witnessing a sub-culture that was not familiar.

Some weird guy, stoned and crazed, offered to share his pot with me. The Midwest was still relatively conservative compared with this more liberal part of the nation. Smoking marijuana so blatantly was not common practice. Politely declining his daring but cordial offer, no way would I have accepted a hit from a stranger off the streets of New York. Besides, I wasn't ready to ignore my traditional values. Although we lived in the same country, I discovered what was the norm in the East was not the norm in every region of our motherland. It was a new world out there!

As the day came to an end, we left the Big Apple and headed back to the Burkes' for another hot meal. Later in the evening, Mr. Burke drove his visitors to JFK airport for the long-awaited exodus. Hugging and thanking our New York keeper, we scattered off to catch the over-night flights. Meri flew in directly from Kansas City for her later connection. After checking luggage and receiving boarding passes, we wandered the corridor for several more hours. Talking and laughing incessantly, I could sense the shared exhilaration we all felt. I was floating on a cloud! Meri and Melody were meeting for the first time as I fretfully awaited their approval of each other. Last-minute phone calls were made to families before getting on the airplanes. Stopping a passerby, I asked him to take a group picture. The man could only speak Spanish. Amused by the exchange, I wasn't even out of the country and I was already encountering a language barrier. Holding up my camera, he knew exactly what I wanted him to do. I thanked him in Spanish.

The time arrived for Mark and me to depart. Melody would leave within the hour and join us in Iceland. Meri was on a different airline and would eventually catch up with us in the city of Luxembourg. Shortly after ten o'clock, our flight lifted off. Butterflies in my stomach were doing the jitter-bug. I'd never felt such elation in my life. There was absolutely no way I would be napping on the plane. Closing my eyes for an instant, I said a little prayer for safe keeping. God speed!

I tried to make small talk with the newlywed couple sitting in the next seat, who proudly announced they were on their honeymoon. As we talked, it didn't take long to realize my oldest brother, Chuck, attended Marine boot camp with the husband. My excursion had only just begun and I was learning what a small world it was in which we lived. Thoroughly enjoying the pleasant conversation with this attractive young couple, certainly made the time pass more quickly.

We arrived in Reykjavik, the capital city of Iceland, after a noisy nine-hour flight. I'm not sure I could have slept even if I wanted to. The plane was not a jet but one of the few prop aircrafts making flights over the ocean. There was a four-hour time difference. Tired but still wound up, Mark and I ate brunch at the hotel while waiting for Mel's later arrival.

After resting a bit, Melody and I took a bus tour offered through the hotel. This islet country was unlike any place I had ever seen. Iceland is the second largest island in Europe.

Renowned as the smokeless city, (and I don't mean cigarettes) Reykjavik is the only city in the whole world heated with natural hot- water flowing from volcanic springs. Although the country is close to the Arctic Circle, the average temperature during the coldest month of January is 30 degrees. Of the 200,000 people who lived in Iceland, about 80,000 of them resided in the great city of Reykjavik.

If there were houses on the moon, this place was probably as close to what I would imagine them to appear. With no visible trees, flowers, or grass, the outside views looked cold and desolate. The summer temperatures averaged around a "balmy" 52 degrees. My lightweight jacket felt good. Plenty of bolder-sized white rocks, geysers, and volcanic mountains were within sight. Most buildings resembled large, gray containers randomly stuck on the side of the hills. Some small goats were tramping about. Even these hairy little creatures were similar in color to their drab surroundings.

Fishing was the main source of revenue for the island's economy. The children learned to fish at young ages. It reminded me of the first time I went fishing with my grandfather when I was only five years old. The only catch of the day was a soft-shelled turtle. Needless to say, my first attempt at fishing was not a success. It's a good thing early failures don't define a person.

The tour guide let his riders know that Iceland has the oldest parliament in existence. He went on to say that in June 1944, the country became an independent republic and was later admitted to the United Nations. This certainly was more information than Melody and I cared to know.

On the bus tour were three American guys traveling with a group of hearing-impaired tourists. Sign language was not a skill I ever acquired, but it may have been much easier to learn than German. Harvey, Dave, and Bernie were accomplished lip readers, and amazingly enough I could talk to them. They would carefully watch our lips and the discussion flowed smoothly. The tour guide lost my undivided attention. A young boy, sitting nearby, joined in the conversations.

Arinbjorn Por Palmason, a twelve-year-old Icelandic student, spoke comprehensible English. He learned his very limited English vocabulary while watching British TV programs. As we chatted, he timidly asked me why my smile made him feel so good. Smiling again, flattered by his sweet, engaging remark, I blushingly thanked him for the compliment. Not sure what else to say to him, I certainly knew my smile would not be the last smile to ever make this young schoolboy feel so good. It didn't take long to realize the people I met along the way would be just as important as the places. I looked forward to making new contacts and taking advantage of my eye-catching smile. My smile would become my best and most influential asset, opening many doors while I traveled.

A variety of bizarre kinds of seafood were served at the hotel restaurant buffet-style dinner. Never in my life had I eaten such an assortment of fish and shellfish recipes. Melody and I sampled shark, squid, whale, smoked puffin, and many other ocean-fed creatures. Most of the morsels tasted scrumptious, but some of the sea urchins were absolutely dreadful.

Growing up in Middle America in the fifties and sixties provided few opportunities for seafood dishes. I was Catholic and used to eating lake water fish, but not fresh water catches. With no seas or oceans close by, seafood was unheard of at most hometown restaurants. Salmon and other fish caught off the coastal waterways were hard to find in Southern Missouri. Transporting frozen fish and seafood across state lines was not widespread during the middle of the century.

After dinner, Melody and I joined some U.S. Navy officials for a drink in the bar. One of the officers was actually the brother of a boy I knew from high school. Hearing he was stationed in Iceland, I made a family contact before leaving the states, hoping to meet him. Officer George Donegan Jr. had flowers and fruit sent to our hotel room. He prearranged a meeting place later in the evening and brought his wife, Stephanie. While visiting this moderately unknown and remote country, we were warmly welcomed by the thoughtfulness of these relative strangers.

Ending up on the dance floor, we danced into the early daybreak hours. The young Icelanders were a rude bunch of dancers! They kept running into each other and shoving us and their partners. Melody was offended by their inconsiderate actions and behavior. This new way of dancing was certainly strange as I noticed this subtle but definite cultural difference. Mark was watching from the side, hanging out with a guy he met from Sweden. Hakan Friberg introduced himself and invited Mel and me to visit him in Stockholm. By three in the morning, I grew weary of the discourteous bar scene. We had no idea how late it was, as daylight loomed outside. Going to bed before dark, even though the time was way after midnight, felt extremely odd.

* * *

Sleeping only a few hours, we hastily ate breakfast rolls and fruit and drank juice in the room. Rushing to catch the airport shuttle, I tried hard to look halfway presentable for the rest of the travel day. While waiting to board the plane, tired and hung over, Melody and I discussed this eccentric place. Neither of us ever cared to revisit this desolate unwelcoming countryside. Settling into my airbus seat, I fumbled with the seatbelt, desperately trying to get the buckle securely fastened. The pain of my throbbing headache began to subside, when this simply gorgeous guy sat down beside me.

Bob Teslow, from Greeley, Colorado, was also headed to Germany. He had just graduated from college and planned to hitchhike and travel in Europe. As we talked and exchanged stories, I found myself feeling sorry for his despondent family life. Trying to be a good listener, my slightly analytical mind surmised he was trying to escape from some pain and searching for his happiness. Traveling alone would never be an option for me, but I admired his bravery. I'm sure others felt admiration for my gutsy endeavor as well. Perhaps I was searching for something more in life too. After all, isn't part of the growing-up process trying to figure out what we want to do with our lives? My impulsive risk taking would also lead me to some answers concerning my own future.

Gazing out the window of the plane, I could see at last we were flying over land. The massive Atlantic Ocean was behind us and below were hundreds of years of history coming into view. I was getting that funny feeling again in the pit of my stomach as I watched the aged buildings move closer to my view. Here is where I would spend the next three months of my life. I wanted to learn as much as I possibly could while roaming these countries where countless well-known people lived before. Their historic legacies paved the roads ahead for my companions and me to discover and explore. Barely able to hide my enthusiasm, I couldn't stop smiling.

Travel was such a classic way to learn about life. The planet was getting smaller. Several of my friends were envious of my going abroad. I don't think I realized at the time what a gift I was receiving. The opportunity presented itself and I took advantage of what I thought anyone would do. Was I a free spirit? I think not! Looking for an exceptional summer, I had the fortitude, and the audacity, to make it all happen. My brothers would disagree and tell you I was just spoiled.

It was nice having Bob to talk to since Melody slept the entire time. As the airplane landed, I wished him the best of luck. Hitchhiking would be risky business! Watching him walk away, I secretly hoped I would see him again. *Wouldn't it be fun to run into him somewhere in Europe?* I thought.

Already deciding my trip was going to be the best, I had no idea there would be so many unusual challenges to face and overcome. Craving new adventure, my optimistic attitude allowed me to reach past the unknown. A close friend once accused me of having "gypsy blood." Excited, and maybe a little worried, I could hardly wait to get going. Life didn't get any better than this!

CHAPTER 1

—

SUNDAY, JUNE 1

Arriving in Luxembourg early evening, Meri was nowhere to be found. She had tried to notify us at the airport, but somehow we missed the page. Going on to the train station, we hoped to find her there. I was concerned. Culture-shocked, by the unfamiliar surroundings and lifestyle, I shuffled about, half dazed. Melody was irritable, totally annoyed at her futile attempts at dialing the telephone. I calmly listened to her ranting and raving.

Tired and cranky from jet lag, we crossed the street from the train station to check in at the Grand Hotel International. To make matters even worse, after signing the guest register, I turned around to pick up my two suitcases and one of them was gone. Franticly, I searched the entire lobby area thinking I would spot the thief with my turquoise Samsonite. Then I panicked and wanted to scream. Now what? How could I survive in Europe for three long months with hardly any money and no clothes? "Thank God," I whispered. "At least I still have my make-up and hair rollers in my overnight case."

I learned fairly quickly what the term "travel light" was all about. Just the previous week, my mom and I had gone shopping for some brand new outfits. Not only would I never see my newest garments again, I hadn't even worn most of them. Upstairs in the room, trying to hold back my tears, I plopped down on the bed. I was feeling sorry for myself, and I got absolutely no sympathy from my comrade, Mark, who shouted and said he trusted this would teach me to be more attentive.

Despite the harsh truth of his words, Mark offered to call the police and report my loss. His German language skills were superior to mine and I welcomed his help with my dilemma. As I was in the midst of my despair, suddenly it dawned on me it was Sunday and I had missed Mass. Caught in the guilt of Catholic-school upbringing, I was forced to confront this regrettable situation. There was absolutely nothing I could do to alter what had just happened. I couldn't let these small inconveniences ruin the rest of my summer. I had to put it behind me and get over it.

The next morning Melody and I decided to go shopping. I needed to buy some new underwear. Peering out the second-story window to inspect the weather conditions outside, I glanced down toward the train station. What a welcome sight! There was lost little Meri, gawking about, while meandering on the sidewalk. I started yelling her name over and over until she looked up to meet my waving hands. Eventually we would have connected at the station, buying tickets to our next destination, but I was extremely happy to see that she was alive and well. My prayers were answered.

Hardly sleeping the night before, I worried about Meri and wondered if she were safe. It turned out that she was okay, and standing close beside her was one fine-looking young man. He was tall, dark, and handsome. Learning he was from Argentina, Meri had met him the preceding evening. Arnaldo Rinlaldi was roving the region. His English was almost perfect.

Most of the foreigners we met could articulate quite well in English. Meri had taken French classes, and Melody and I both had Spanish in high school. Exchanging addresses and work information, Arnaldo planned to make a stopover in Germany before the end of the month.

The first thing we had to do was exchange currency before running errands. I bought a youth hostel card, which allowed discounts on certain room rentals, and then we purchased train tickets to Paris. Melody left that afternoon. She was spending one night with some people she worked with in Houston who were vacationing in France. Meri and I would leave the next day to join her. Mark headed to Hildesheim, Germany, to advance his language studies. He teased me about not liking beer since I would be spending my summer in a country that is best known for its ale. We talked about getting together again during the summer, but that was the last time I ever saw Mark.

Meri and I set out to see a few attractions. Luxembourg is the capital of the Grand Duchy and over a thousand years old. The country is trilingual, speaking Luxembourgish, German, and French. We did hear several languages spoken as we walked the streets. Allegedly, this older municipality is the "land of haunted castles."

We wandered into Saint Michael's Church, where the wooden panels in the entryway boasted elaborate paintings. Ornate frescoes of early saints and religious figures covered the walls. This was the first of many, many more ancient and glorious churches we would see throughout the summer.

Returning to the lodge after a long day of sight-seeing, as we entered the foyer, Meri set her travel case in a chair. She had just turned away when it was stolen right out from under her nose. This time we caused a scene at the front desk. The staff was not amused at our upsetting drama, though. We were mad and feeling violated as guests in a hotel that was frequented by thieves! Once again, authorities were called, drawing attention to this establishment and the robberies taking place. In Meri's shoulder bag were some books, her return airline ticket, and traveler's checks. She had to immediately reinstate her lost currency. For such a small country, it sure had a major crime problem. The charm and allure were rapidly losing appeal. We were ready to get the heck out.

* * *

What a nightmare the first few days had been, and our stay wasn't over yet. After packing and eating breakfast, we hurried to the train station through drizzly rain. While sitting in the noisy waiting room, unable to hear the Paris departure announcement, we missed the coach to France. It would be five long hours before the next train to Paris. Cashing in our tickets, we decided to wing it. Meri observed young people hitchhiking, both guys and gals, and thought we should give it a whirl. Besides, there was no way we were staying five more hours in that criminal place. It didn't take long to get a ride. The rain may have helped our case, but I'm sure it had more to do with our sex. Maybe we just got lucky? Whatever the reason, we were truly grateful for the two youthful U.S. Air Force men who took pity and stopped their miniature European automobile for us.

Stuffed in a white Triumph like sardines, Dave Lynch and Rick Wolf offered to drive the way to Paris. They were stationed in Hunsruck, Germany, and on leave for a few days. We invited them to join our Paris tour. How could they not accept? Approaching the metropolitan area, the traffic turned absolutely horrific. Driving through a round-about for the first time was a harrowing experience. The circle was six to eight lanes deep with drivers honking their horns and making obscene hand gestures. I wasn't even driving, but I was a nervous wreck just navigating.

As expected, we had trouble finding the hotel where Melody was staying. In the vicinity was Hotel Telst, which advertised its three-dollar rooms for a night. What a deal! Around the corner was the illustrious Arc De Triomphe. This monument honored those who fought for France in wars. Beneath the arch is the tomb of their unknown soldier from WW I. After check-in, we went to eat at an old-world French restaurant. The menu wasn't in English and I ordered something I was not expecting. It looked like raw strips of bacon laid over various salad greens. Big mistake!

By the time we finished eating, the day had gotten away from us. In the cozy ambiance of the hotel room, Mel and I talked about childhood outings. Our fathers worked for the same company in Oklahoma, and we met as little girls. Living in Tulsa since birth, my dad was transferred after I finished kindergarten.

Melody grew up in Muskogee and we got together over summer vacations. Before going to sleep, Melody confided she and her boyfriend were questioning whether to continue their relationship. She had to get away to think about their future togetherness. Trying to empathize, I fully agreed that the temporary separation would help with her decision making. Meri also offered some sound advice. Counseling sessions among friends was cheap therapy!

Discussing the trip goals, we wanted to see and do as much as we could fit into the summer. Melody was okay with whatever we decided in travel plans. She was along for the diversion and trusted any decisions made in the itinerary. A silver guide booklet filled with information would become a bible as we continually checked out places of interest and things to do. The pamphlet noted historic landmarks, hotels, shops, restaurants, and seasonal events in the well-known cities.

Without hesitation, we girls were frequently recognized as North American tourists. Maybe it was our more western dress apparel, compared to the tightly worn European attire. Who knew? Wearing our in style miniskirts did cause some heads to turn. The three of us gals were about the same size in weight and height: five feet plus a few inches with various shades and lengths of long, blond hair. Looking enough alike, we probably could have passed for sisters. Fortunately for me, we could wear each other's clothes. Good friends come in handy during times of undress.

Meri was knowledgeable about France, learning most of this information in her language class. Paris, the capital and largest city in the country, is like no other. I'd heard about Paris all my life and I was totally thrilled to be in the notorious city. Numerous historic buildings lined the grand boulevards. In this world center of art and culture were many museums, theaters, shops, and cafés. We quickly learned one new Franc equaled twenty cents and the hotels and restaurants customarily added a service charge to most billings. Constantly calculating prices in our heads, we tallied the checks and split the costs three ways. No gourmet meals were allowed on our limited budget.

Looking ahead and thinking about stretching funds over the long summer, Meri was rather frugal, I was very practical, and Melody was the carefree spender. There was nothing we could afford to buy in those pricey boutiques and exclusive shops. However, limited resources didn't stop our looking. We'd enjoy as much as possible in this thoroughly seductive city. After all, we were in Paris!

The following morning, Rick, Meri, and I ventured out to the Left Bank. We were hunting for a place to stay that was more student-friendly. It took forever to find a discounted hotel on Saint Michelle Boulevard. Rick dropped us off and went back for Melody and Dave and the rest of the gear. Compact vehicles were not the most convenient for five adult travelers. The morning faded fast, as our walking tour eventually materialized. We were in the midst of their artistic heritage.

In the heart of the city along the River Seine was the twelfth-century Notre Dame Cathedral. This miraculous old church, dedicated to "Our Lady," was one of the first Gothic cathedrals. The extremely high walls supported the raised ceilings. Continuing through the very formal Tuileries Garden Park, we passed Rue de la Paix, one of the high-priced shopping districts. Gazing up at the Saint-Jacques decorated tower monument, we entered the divine Church of Sainte-Chapelle and marveled at the kaleidoscope of the many beautiful stained-glass windows. The multicolored panes covered most of the interior wall. Eventually we found our way to the Palais du Louvre Museum, located on the Right Bank of the River Seine. It was an absolute whirlwind of a morning. The guys had to run off, duty calling them back to the barracks. We owed them a debt of gratitude for patiently accommodating the needs of three scattered females with too much stuff.

The Louvre is a central landmark in Paris and the world's most visited art museum. This historic shrine holds a collection of more than thirty-thousand objects. There was a remarkable assortment of artifacts, from the prehistoric period to the nineteenth century. This showplace of art included ancient Egyptian, Etruscan, Greek, and Roman relics. Hand-carved statues, enamels, ceramics, and jewels filled the various departments as we hurried to the hall of oil prints and drawings.

We inspected countless over-studied paintings, too many to mention in this text. But everyone's favorite was Leonardo da Vinci's critically acclaimed, the elegant *Mona Lisa*, with her mysterious smile. We paced leisurely through the halls, reading the artists' names under each piece. The lives of these men were as intriguing as their work. If the paint and marble could talk, I can't imagine the priceless stories we might have heard. Sadly, some of these artists' lives we know nothing about.

* * *

After a few Kodak moments, and stopping for a late lunch at an outdoor cafe, the afternoon began with a stroll through the Latin Quarter. This selective, artsy district near the Sorbonne University includes many bistros and restaurants. Typically, students in Bohemian attire gathered around. In close proximity was the original Bastille, the prison where the French Revolution began in 1789. Everywhere we looked were exceptional flowering gardens and flowing fountains. We spent hours inspecting the novel books, amateur prints, and artists.

Two men from North Africa were kind enough to show us the way to the University of Paris. Along the avenue was a tall, tower-like fountain. The unusual monument was in memory of the many battles fought for France during their wars. Several of Napoleon's victories were noted. Napoleon Bonaparte was considered the greatest military and political leader of modern times. This influential man controlled most of Europe in the early 1800s. After the French Revolution, the supreme commander died in exile when he was only fifty-one years old.

With sunset imminent, we were restless to see the most stirring landmark in the romantic city. Stepping off the Metro, I immediately saw the Eiffel Tower in all of its grandeur. Wow! Built in 1889 for the Paris Exhibition, the tower is over a thousand feet tall with three levels to see the views. This iron formation is the tallest building in Paris and named after the designer engineer. The construction was magnificent and the sparkle of the dazzling lights illuminated the dark sky. I couldn't get over the large numbers of tourists and spectators milling around. It was marvelous!

We met a darling French boy on the Metro named Alain Cruz, who offered to show us to the plaza. He was about ten or so and his English was limited. This didn't stop him from hanging out, with three older women. Several more inquisitive men came around. Most could not speak any English so I'd smile and shrug my shoulders. Meri tried to utter a few greetings in French. Our efforts became laughable and we chuckled at the botched attempts talking to one another. *What a memorable day in the world's much-loved city*, I thought, as I sat mesmerized by the glittery glow surrounding me.

Viewing Paris after dark made a late night out and prevented an early start to our last tour day. A rather strange thing happened on the way to the Metro. As we walked down the sidewalk, a peculiar-looking man stopped in our path, passing out coupons for a free visit to his health and beauty clinic. He claimed to be doing research on a treatment for the reduction of fat cells. That certainly sparked our interest! Like most younger women, we believed you could never be too rich or too thin. He offered a quick demonstration if we had ten minutes to spare. Sure!

Gullible by nature and innocent in age, we eagerly followed this squatty, chubby man to his office. As we climbed the back stairs of an old, dilapidated building, I was starting to have doubts about his so-called "miracle claim." Was this guy for real or were we being taken for fools? Mel had recently gained weight and volunteered to be the first guinea pig. She willingly stepped up on the exam table as the witch doctor took a hand full of white cream from a jar and rubbed it on her upper thighs. Now I was convinced he was some sort of quack and we'd fallen for his bogus trick. Leaving abruptly, we dashed down the staircase, giggling all the way to the street. Boy, were we embarrassed! And yes, we were fools, falling hook, line, and sinker for such a ludicrous story.

Searching for the train station, we needed to buy tickets to Germany. A summer Eurail pass cost one-hundred dollars. We discussed how easy it was to get rides as well as the money we would save. Meri suggested forgetting the pass and continue to hitchhike. Besides, we would miss out on some local cultural neighborhoods if we stayed on the train. With the extra cash saved, we made a beeline to the outdoor flea market to do a little barter shopping.

While inspecting the bargains, two distinguished-looking middle-aged Englishmen walked over to talk and offered to buy our lunch. These smartly attired gentlemen seemed nice enough, so we consented. Over a glass of wine with tomato bisque and fresh vegetable salads, these men proceeded to divulge more French history than I could possibly absorb.

The lessons were enlightening and Meri was benefiting from the reviews. Melody, on the other hand, was yawning with boredom. After a few glasses of wine she'd get fairly silly and flirtatious. The merlot made Meri even chattier. Trying to pay polite attention, my mind was fading fast. After one glass of wine I was transformed into complete relaxation. In my tranquility, glancing around the table, I realized the drinks had made everyone happy. Cheers to red, red wine!

After lunch, the men offered to reveal some out-of-the-way places. Meri quickly accepted, approving of these well-versed guides. John and Roger lead the way to Basilica du Sacre Coeur at Montmartre. Towering high on a hill was a massive Catholic Church of Romano-Byzantine architecture. Gothic cathedrals and Romanesque-style churches of the Renaissance period ruled these territories. As night descended, the City of Lights became bright with all the glitz and Ritz.

Once again, these generous men indulged us with an extended meal in a classy French cuisine restaurant. While eating, I enjoyed listening to the pair, gaining knowledge from their vast experiences. As we finished off dessert, the educated duo recommended seeing the opera-ballet. Opera wasn't especially my style of music, but in Paris, opera would most fittingly conclude the sensational day. Leaving the restaurant, we took a taxi to the Palais Garnier opera house. The Opéra de Paris was the most decorative theatrical structure I'd ever seen. Even the chandeliers were enchantingly ornamental. Everything was exceptional and the evening extravaganza would not have been possible without the generosity of our sophisticated escorts. What a magical night!

Booking a bus tour from the hotel, we traveled to Versailles the following day. On the ten-mile trip outside of town, the coach passed Concord Square, where during the French Revolution, a guillotine was erected. Along with many others, Queen Marie Antoinette lost her head there in front of cheering crowds. We passed by another impressive point of interest: A memorial of Joan of Arc on a golden horse was in Palace des Pyramides. Sitting next to me was an intriguing man from Lebanon. Albert Ghazelian from Beirut let me know he worked for Mercedes-Benz in his own country.

The Palace was like a fairy tale castle, built in the fifteenth century during the celebrated reign of Louis the XIV. This large building and decorations were his greatest architectural undertaking. Enjoyed by many kings and queens, this brilliant fortress, with the ceilings and walls covered by incredible paintings, was definitely fitting for the royalty that once lived there. The most popular room, inspired by King Louis XIV, was the lavish Galerie des Glaces or the Hall of Mirrors. We stood in the corridor where the time-honored Versailles Treaty was signed after World War I.

The community of Versailles was used as a model for the building of our own Washington, D.C. Outside in the gardens were flowers of every variety in a multitude of radiant colors. The landscape was in classic French garden style with meticulously manicured lawns. Beautiful flowing water fountains were on display and standing alone was the French Statue of Liberty. This gift, from America, was given to France after the French gave the Statue of Liberty to our country. The gardeners and caretakers diligently worked as we soaked up the loveliness.

On the bus ride back to town, I stared out the window and felt sad that our time in Paris was about over. The fashionable French styles of clothes were beyond my means but worth the pleasure of seeing what I used to view only in the magazines. Fashion, the universal language! I watched the women, prancing along the footpath, in their striking textured fabrics and collection of trendy prints. Shaken back to reality, we passed by an outdoor lavatory situated on their sidewalk. Yuk!

Thinking back to my formative junior high school days, while babysitting for the Marx family, after I put the kids to bed I'd browse through *Vogue* and *Harper's Bazaar* wish books. Most of the outfits I would never wear, but I could daydream the hours away, while waiting on the parents to return home. Looking at the glamorous clothes and hair styles, I convinced myself the designer wears were not fitting for my dumpy body. Most professional models were nearly six feet tall. My fairly moderate tastes were more down to earth. Thinking I was reserved and boring, I often wished to be more daring.

Watching these foreign people and hearing their charming accents was captivating, despite my feeling that most of the French people were not friendly. A couple of times we had to ask for directions and they acted as if they couldn't understand. *Bonjour*, we knew better!

Exploring this splendid city, we were able to sample a smidgen of all the delights that the world had to offer. In Paris, one could find the plain taste of a sweet piece of chocolate or observe the delicate atmosphere of an expensive boutique. Paris did excel, whether by the hand of nature or by the many talents and creative works of their citizens. There was no scarcity of nice-looking men, and I was not opposed to looking at God's creations. European men seemed different, much less inhibited than the men I knew back in America. Although I was extremely self-conscious, watching these men brought a smile to my face as I thought about the remaining days of summer.

Getting up early to catch the morning train, there was a misunderstanding at check-out. Consequently, we didn't arrive at the station in a timely manner. Another missed connection! This train travel was becoming increasingly frustrating. However, hitchhiking into Germany was not recommended by most travelers. The Germans were more strict at the borders with passport checks and screenings. We also heard it was against the law to hitchhike on the highways. We certainly didn't want to take any chances.

To pass time, before the afternoon train, we set out for an art exhibit at the Petit Palace Hotel. Later we came across a building containing museums and monuments relating to the military history of France. Inside Les Invalides, we discovered the tomb of Napoleon and the burial places of his other family members. Under the brilliant dome in this complex structure is the elaborate gravesite of this one-time emperor of the French. His outstanding and celebrated rule lasted more than ten long years before his defeat in Belgium at the Battle of Waterloo.

In the courtyard outside the building, a wedding was commencing. Melody followed the crowds and the guests into the church of Eglise du Dome. No one tried to stop our intrusion, or if they did, we didn't know. We proceeded to crash the wedding. The marriage party included women in stylish satin gowns and well-groomed men in black tuxes. Standing in the back of the church as an uninvited guest, I listened to the familiar music while I watched the couples parade down the aisle. The aroma of fresh-cut flowers and pungent perfumes filled the elegant chapel. Disappointedly, we didn't have time to stay for the reception and champagne toast.

Missing another train, God forbid, wouldn't be worth the free cake and petit fours. Abruptly leaving the church, I said *adieu* to France and *merci* for everything. We darted off once again to the station. Quickly boarding the train, we had few minutes to spare.

The ride through Germany was lengthy and uneventful. Sitting next to me was a young couple from Frankfurt. They tried to be helpful in answering my numerous questions about the town. After arriving, they pointed to where we caught the last bus of the evening going to the hotel. By the time we reached employee housing, all the doors were locked. At the hotel registration desk, I presented my confirmation letter and we were allowed to check into a guest room for the night.

I greeted the workers in German, and everyone spoke to me in English. One of the staff told me the grammar-school children were required to take seven years of English-language classes. As

I tried practicing my new verbal skills, the guy at the front desk asked me to speak English so he could understand me better. After his rude comment, I asked myself why I bothered taking that unspeakable German class. *Oh, well, at least I would be able to read street signs and order my meals in Deutsch*, I thought. I had to think positively! Expressing my appreciation, I said "danke schoen" to the clerk and picked up my one suitcase. The bellman offered no help as he pointed to the service elevator and said it was mandatory for employees to use the back door.

The hotel, a noted four-star establishment, was situated next to the Frankfurt am Main Airport and the American Rhein-Main Air Base. The military base was used as the arrival and departure facility for U.S. Army troops, so most of the guests were Americans. This very large facility was so Americanized that it was hard to tell we were in another country. In our large single room were two double beds and a separate bathroom. However, unlike in the States, there was a bidet in the restroom. Great for washing dirty feet! It was certainly a step up from the cheap hotel room we rented while staying in Paris. For a few days, at least, we would be living in the lap of luxury.

Even the toilets flushed like the ones we were used to back home. Almost every toilet we'd encountered had an unusual flushing apparatus. Some restrooms had a chain you pulled from the ceiling, while others had a button on the floor you pressed with your foot. Some tanks had a knob directly on top that you had to push. The toilet tissue was also an immeasurable improvement compared with the rough, crepe-paper-textured rolls in the Paris hotel. You get what you pay for!

Frankfurt, Germany

CHAPTER 2

—

SUNDAY, JUNE 8

I was up bright and early to report to work. Administration was off, and we were told to come back Monday morning. Now they tell us! I voted to go back to bed, but Meri was ready to go into the city. She wanted to see this town where we'd be living the next few months. Grabbing the guide brochures and map, we headed out for a day in the downtown district. Before getting on the bus, we had to patiently wait for a soccer team to unload. Watching the athletic bunch of German football players was like having a personal pre-game show. Go black, red, and gold!

Germany is considered the heart of Europe. After World War II ended in 1945, the western part of the country formed the federal Republic of Germany. Frankfurt, a significant industrial city, has a wealth of international traffic. During the war, much of the city was destroyed. Today it is the largest financial and transportation center in Germany. It was obviously a bustling center for commerce, and from the bus window I was able to see the many stores and businesses along its very modern streets. On the long ride into town, Meri read some interesting facts from the tour booklet. Johann Wolfgang Von Goethe, a well-known

German poet, was born in Frankfurt and the oldest university in Frankfurt was named for this key figure in German literature.

Jumping off the bus in an area called Sachsenhausen, we viewed a neighborhood that is still preserved like the "old town" style of buildings. Appealing shops, sundries, pubs, and eateries were left in their traditional German-style architecture. Their monetary currency was the deutsche mark, or the D-mark. The exchange rate of approximately four marks to the dollar provided another easy conversion, as I priced items in my head when thinking of potential purchases. Making time for a Sunday break after the walking and window shopping, I started looking for a church to attend Mass. Similar to Paris, there seemed to be countless old churches, one on every street corner. Turning down a cobblestone lane away from the business section, we walked toward a house of worship. Hearing the sounds of a familiar Latin song coming through the opened windows, the parishioners sang loudly. Peeking through the huge doors, we tiptoed in and slid into the pew while the service was in progress at St. Bartholomeus, Imperial Cathedral.

After Mass, we took a hike through a nearby park. Three Italian guys followed behind us, trying to make conversation. Their English was not great and we spoke no Italian. Laboring to talk to them, I asked how they came to work in Germany. One of the guys, Apollo, tried to tell me that young aspiring waiters will work in several different countries throughout Europe. After learning three or four languages over several years, they will eventually go back to Italy to be well-versed servers. Being able to speak to tourists in their own language was important to them. The job of a male waiter in Italy is considered a respected profession, a career choice. Most American men wouldn't consider this type of occupation, except temporarily, while working their way through school. Impressed by their ardent dedication, I let them know it was highly commendable.

The guys joined us for a bite to eat at a German fast-food canteen. In these self-service eating places, you ordered food at the counter and ate while standing up next to high tables. Eating without sitting was cheaper since we avoided the added gratuity. I couldn't help but notice the attendants seldom smiled when taking orders. I'd heard that Germans were cold and calculated, showing few outward emotions. After the quick lunch, we took a relaxed tour of the luscious Palmengarten. The botanical garden was overflowing with lovely tropical and subtropical plants.

With evening approaching, the Italians directed our course to the Black Jack nightclub for dancing. Surprisingly, many American records were being played. Current songs by Janis Joplin, Bob Dylan, Jimi Hendrix, and Creedence Clearwater Revival blasted the room. Every other song was a record by my favorite group, the Beatles. We flirted with smiles and glances as interested men came up to converse with us; the music was too loud for me to talk over anyway. Preferring rock 'n' roll, without talking, I was on the dance floor the remainder of the night.

Reporting to work the next morning, for the second time, most of the day was spent filling out forms and signing requisite paperwork. Mrs. Diebecker, the lady in charge of housekeeping, opened the utility closet and gave thorough instructions on how to use the cleaning products. This short, somber woman wore a murky-colored, martial-like uniform, matching her severe demeanor. From her ruthless expressions, it was clear she was one tough lady who would not put up with any childish nonsense. Confiscating our passports, she affirmed they would be returned once work visas were issued. Melody gave her a salute as she turned and walked away. The good news was that all three of us had jobs at the hotel for the summer. Thank you, Lord!

Some of the other staff members introduced themselves. There were students from Denmark, Italy, France, Holland, and Germany. Only two other girls were from the United States, Annette and Rosalind. During our lunch break we were permitted to go to the employee dining room, where we found out the scoop on the strict working conditions, the numerous rules, and endless regulations.

The meal didn't look too appetizing. German potatoes, pork, and hard bread were served cafeteria-style. I was the first to grumble about the greasy food. Obsessed about gaining weight, it had only been a few years since I'd lost thirty-two pounds, and I was picky about what I ate. Mrs. Diebecker, the *Hausdame*, marched over to our table, giving orders to report to work at six o'clock sharp. Quickly losing my appetite, I nearly chocked after hearing how early I'd have to get up in the mornings.

Employee dorm rooms weren't complete for move-in, so we stayed another night at the hotel. Apparently, the maid on duty complained about our cluttered room and we were instructed to go tidy up. Only paying customers received maid service. Going back to clean the room, I turned on the television to a British news channel. While cleaning, we listened to current news events in Europe and back in the states. President Nixon had just met with South Vietnam's leader, Nguyen Van Thieu, announcing U.S. troop withdrawals from Vietnam to begin within thirty days. By the end of the summer, twenty-five thousand American soldiers would be headed home. This good news was a relief since everyone knew someone who'd been killed in the extensive conflict.

After room clean-up, we boarded the bus again and went back to town. Lots of guys came up to talk. The attention was nice, but there were times when I preferred to be left alone to look and shop. My girlfriends and I were becoming increasingly curious as to why we were singled out by these European men. They seemed to know we were Americans before we said a word. Melody was glad she wasn't mistaken for a German; she wanted to be recognized as an all-American girl. Sometimes Meri pretended she couldn't understand English, shaking her head perplexed when someone spoke to her. But they weren't fooled. I thought maybe our not being smokers was a giveaway. Most of the youth had cigarettes in their possessions. Smoking was one bad habit we didn't have in common.

Since I wasn't a "morning person," getting up at five was for the birds. To try to get some additional rest, I washed my hair the night before. With only one restroom for three girls to share, sometimes we were all in the bathroom at the same time. Daily shampooing and inserting big wire-brush hair curlers was a nightly chore. The absolute worst part of the whole day was getting out of bed.

On the first full day of work, German-issued, dark-brown uniforms were distributed. These jumper-style dresses worn over short-sleeved cotton blouses were covered with a white linen apron. Pantyhose had to be worn at all times. Cleaning rooms and washing out toilets in those hideous chambermaid outfits made absolutely no sense. Thank heaven we didn't have to wear those crimpy little hats. But, to add insult to more humiliation, we had to work alone and no talking was allowed while on duty. I didn't dare question my authority but I sure wanted to ask if it was O.K. to speak to a guest if spoken to. I was incensed. The thought of working in silence, and by myself, was not what I was expecting for my summer vacation. How unreasonable!

After a brief training session, we were assigned rooms for scrubbing and sent out to swab, rub, scour, brush, dust, and polish. Being a *zimmermachen* (room maid) was not going to be pleasant. Melody poked fun at the way we looked in our maid costumes. I was humiliated! The Germans were notorious for their hard work and this was one team I was not wild about joining. What had I done? I apologized to my friends for getting them into this deplorable situation. Not that I minded working but I didn't like working alone. Isolation was mentally unhealthy and it sure wasn't fun.

Dinner hour became our happy hour. Looking forward to eating at the end of each day gave me time to unwind and socialize. The communal gathering together amidst food and friends was worth the long wait until supper. Humor became medicinal as we talked and snickered about the occupational hazards. Grievance complaints and whining were primary topics. What a life!

How was I going to make it through the whole summer getting up at the crack of dawn? These people were so regimented and the work load so urgent. One early afternoon, we were sent to the employee clinic. A partial physical, including a chest X-ray, a urine sample, and blood tests, was required. Melody questioned the necessity of these invasive procedures. Meri teased that maybe we were an experimental group for "the perfect maids." Sensing the German arrogance from the staff, the nurses showed absolutely no empathy in their treatment protocol and Meri nearly passed out. After several hours of waiting, and a big bruise on my arm, we were finally allowed to leave. Too late to go back to work after that gruesome ordeal, we needed to decompress. Taking a relaxing walk in the woods near the hotel was just what the doctor ordered. The late afternoon sun was warm and a cool breeze lifted the hot air. Lying down on the soft ground, I closed my eyes and pondered medieval times. *Knights in white armor surely rode through this Bavarian forest*, I thought.

On the way back to the room, we were startled by a visit from Arnaldo, the guy who rescued Meri the night she was lost in Luxembourg. I honestly didn't think he would come to see us. After an informative visit, he sincerely hoped we could meet again as our traveling time allowed. It was not to be. We were never able to fit a trip into our schedule with this nice young man.

Eventually we moved our possessions from the hotel to employee housing. Assigned to totally different roommates, we requested switching around to the same room. The little apartment was sparsely furnished and confined. A small nightstand separated two twin beds on one side of the long, narrow room and built-in metal lockers lined the other side of the living space. The walls were constructed of concrete blocks. Looking more like a prison cell, post-Nazi Germany hadn't progressed much in present-day decorating styles. Promptly moving a third bed into the double room, we were forced to do some minor rearranging. Any alteration was a major improvement to the reform-school atmosphere. Our monotonous room needed some thoughtful creativity.

Mess hall was a much livelier spot than the sleeping quarters. The younger Germans were not as controlled as the senior citizens. Sometimes I would watch them while they ate, paying close attention to their impeccable table manners. The kids from other countries were more relaxed and easier to make conversation. Most of the new friends we were making, were not from Germany.

Joining our table for supper the first week was a lovable French boy named Chris Yzquierdo, a proud Italian named Bruno

Suetoni, and his friend, Franco. The gregarious trio was a bit pushy but funny, and their slight physiques posed no real threat of intimidation. Before the meal was finished, we received an invitation to go dancing on Friday night in a neighboring discotheque. Needing to get away from the physical abuse of manual labor, I was ready for some much needed diversion.

* * *

Work was not always lonesome. One busy day, the manager allowed us to work in pairs. A Canadian girl named Margaret was my assigned partner. I noticed early on that European girls didn't shave their legs or under their armpits. Tactfully inquiring about this atypical hygiene practice, I brought up the subject of shaving. Margaret wasn't insulted and told me only prostitutes shaved. It wasn't customary for most European women to shave. And the men didn't find these hairy legs offensive. How gross! However, after hearing this, I was almost tempted to forgo shaving the remainder of the summer. It sure would make life easier and one less thing I would have to do in the mornings while getting ready for work. Not that I preferred being a "wild woman."

Still trying to spruce up the apartment, we bought giant posters and white candles from the lobby gift shop. The pictures were beautiful mountain scenes, adding a lift to the otherwise dull room. Decorating the bare walls with the giant photographs made our living space more tolerable.

Melody thought it would be nice to invite our new friends over for an evening card party. The candles added a soft light to the studio dwelling. Meri fluffed the bed pillows, faking a couch-like appearance. The guys offered to bring their portable record player and forty-fives to provide the music. With everyone's ingenuity and input, we had everything we needed for the gathering. With no chairs to sit around the small table, we lounged on the beds to play cards. The evening was invigorating with this culturally diverse group of kids. Everyone talked as best they could, given the tongue-tied circumstances. Each person spoke his or her own language with limited use of other languages they knew. Most could speak some English with a little German,

Italian, and French thrown in. Having so much fun, we decided to do it again the very next night. Anything to help make the intense working conditions bearable was worth the extra efforts. I hated my job!

As the days turned into a week, my feet were feeling the abuse. After work I just wanted to sit with my feet propped up. Beginning another sundown card game, we received a phone call from management supervision. Someone blew the whistle! It was against house rules for the opposite sex to congregate in each other's room. Told to behave like good little children, we had to kick out the boys. Like good little girls, we did what we were told and proceeded to throw a fit. The unfair treatment was uncalled for and the restrictions irrational. Was this not ridiculous?

Mail was handed out the end of each day. Receiving a note from home, enclosed in the letter, was a confirmation notice for a job offer in Switzerland. Beginning the fifth of July through the end of August, there would be two positions available at the Hotel Krone. Showing the memo to the girls, I recommended we leave Germany and check out this place for employment. The work couldn't possibly be any worse and I didn't want to spend another month in this holding camp. The more we talked about the potential move, the more enthused we became. By the end of the month, after getting paid, a decision was made to move on from here. I could hardly wait!

Saturday morning, a well-deserved day off, we slept until noon. Staying out late Friday, we went dancing at the Jim Bean Club with Chris, Bruno, and another Italian named Angelo. Missing morning kitchen hours, we ate a "continental breakfast" in the room as a mealtime alternative. While sitting on the bed eating hard rolls with orange marmalade jam, Melody suggested we go out and sunbath. Our white legs and pale faces needed attention. Avid sun worshipers, we thought our brown skin made us look healthier. The warmth of the hot sun felt wonderful and I had no idea how much damage I was doing to my skin. Homemade sun screen consisted of baby or coconut oil mixed with iodine. The darker the tan, the better I looked, and we spent several hours soaking up the ultraviolet rays.

After a few hours of baking, another trip into town ensued. Getting off the bus at Saxon Avenue, we walked alongside the Rhine-Main River that flows through Frankfurt. On a mission, we were in search of a street named Kaiserstrasse, where the prostitutes hung out. Prostitution was legal and we were curious to see how these women worked. Easily recognized, their shaved legs, short skirts, and pointy stiletto high heels made them highly visible. Most of the girls were attractive, and I was baffled that they needed to make their income in this demeaning way. Maybe they thought working as chambermaids was equally as demeaning?

A well-dressed man in a dark suit walked up and asked in German, "How much"? He was obviously an American and mortified when we told him in plain English that we were not for sale. Apologizing profusely, he said he was on business from St. Louis, Missouri. After that blunder, Melody decided we didn't need to hang around any longer. Meri was tickled pink that someone actually considered paying for her. I teased her to keep on shaving those shapely legs.

Not long after the proposition, three U.S. military guys came up and introduced themselves. We reassured them we were not trying to make any extra money. They invited us to go with them to the NCO Club at the Rhein-Main Air Base. Anything would be better than street walking and being mistaken for hookers. Squeezing into their extremely packed vehicle, we drove away from the tricks of the trade in the very active and busy metropolis.

After arriving at the NCO club, the guys were denied admittance due to dress blue requirements. Three other uniformed men offered to usher our entry. Lenny, Sam, and Gary became our dates at the dance hall. Listening to a zippy Irish band, we ate, talked, and danced up a storm into the early morning hours. We told our newly acquired friends about the incarceration at work, and they sympathetically said we could move into their pad. *What a deal*, I thought, *cook and clean their place with no rules or restrictions. Right*! Flippantly, but politely, I refused their informal proposal.

The enjoyable and amusing evening with these fine young officers eventually came to an end. They requested our company for another night of entertainment and dancing the following weekend. Looking at Meri and Mel, receiving nods of approval, I had to assume they were having as much fun as I was having. By the time we got back to the dorm, it was way past three in the morning.

Although the Air Force trio were not the debonair European men we were expecting to meet, they were humorous and might have been cool to hang out with. At least we all spoke the same language and were close in age. There was a certain comfort level I felt being around guys my own age. Talking to older men was not as easy. I lacked a mature social confidence and in some ways I felt inadequate. With these guys, I wouldn't fret as much about how I looked or acted.

I'm not really sure why we agreed so easily to meet them again. Perhaps we felt protected and secure because they were United States military. I often wondered why certain people came into my life when they did. Sometimes a person left my life as fast as he or she entered it, but I would remember the person forever. These guys literally picked us up right off the street, and we would spend a good deal of time with them over the remainder of the month in Frankfurt. The days were getting better and I was thankful for the variety of people we were meeting and the new friends we were making. Maybe it wouldn't be so bad in Germany after all!

CHAPTER 3

—

SUNDAY, JUNE 15

As much as I wanted to sleep in, I got up for Sunday Mass. Meri joined me, as we sluggishly rode the bus into town and attended services at St. Mary's. Initially, it was hard to know if we were in a Catholic church or a Lutheran church. In this country, where the Protestant Reformation began, there were fifty-million Lutherans and twenty-five-million Catholics in Germany. The worship services were very similar, except that the Catholics were always crossing themselves.

I seldom grew tired of seeing the magnificent Romanesque and Baroque-style cathedrals. Every piece of artwork, whether a painting, sculpture, or religious statue, was a masterpiece. One would have to presume with no television, movie theaters, or radios for amusement, the men had to keep busy doing something. Many artists were commissioned to build the Christian churches with spacious interiors that had to be filled with colorful decorations. I was certainly envious of the talent. I could barely draw a stickman. Speaking of which, a German school for painting had flourished in Frankfurt in the 1500s and 1600s. The artistes were expertly trained!

While walking around the city, I pondered on these unyielding German people and how their country had been under a dictatorship and military occupation for nearly twenty years. Now two decades later, everything changed. It had to be difficult for their nation to accept the democratic procedures.

Growing up in a free country allowed me to be an independent thinker. No wonder these people were not as free and spontaneous as their government permitted them to be. Knowing communism still existed across their border to the east would have to make one nervous. You could see the anguish and distress in the faces of the older generation. It was hard for me to relate to their agony, never having lived through the horrors of such a destructive war and the unbelievable dismay of the holocaust.

Every other week, afternoon shifts were assigned. Evenings were slower, and there was more time to visit one another while working. Swiping wrapped crackers, butter, and jelly packs off the food trays left in the halls, we'd eat and chit-chat while on a break. Not caring anymore if I got into trouble, I had a bad attitude. Meri would go over our getaway plans for the next day off and Melody would often imitate the overly stuffy management. In a few short weeks we'd be leaving and we looked forward to a better life and work situation. Probably the only reason I wasn't very depressed was because I knew the torment would soon be over. There was light at the end of the month!

Turning twenty on June sixteenth, I didn't feel much like celebrating. For some reason, this passage into young adulthood was causing me pain and suffering. No longer a teenager but still feeling like an adolescent in many ways, I missed my younger years. Leaving my childhood behind, I could only think about how I'd have to be more accountable and more responsible. What a miserable thought! Grieving the loss of my youth, I wasn't quite ready to be grown up.

Claudio Gasparini, one of the good-looking Italian waiters, invited me over for dinner. He fixed spaghetti from some leftovers he was able to confiscate from the hotel restaurant kitchen. Trying to create a romantic atmosphere in his room, he placed a white table cloth, candles, and a single red rose, on the bedside stand. As hard as he tried to cheer me up, I just wanted to pout. No other birthday affected me the same way as letting go of my teenage years.

The following afternoon we had lunch at Palm Gardens with our new Air Force buds. I was in a better frame of mind since my birthday was over. Lenny Genovese, a short extrovert from New York, spoke with a strong Eastern U.S. accent, complimenting his outgoing personality. Capturing my shyness with his allure, Lenny encouraged me to come out of my shell. Gary Stafford, tall and slim, wore horn-rimmed glasses that shadowed his good looks. He and Melody became fast friends. Sam had a girlfriend back in the States and was not as interested in socializing. Lenny and Gary, budding comics, laughed more at their own jokes then we did. The conversations centered on our coordinating a trip together, time permitting. These guys were willing to visit other parts of Germany. Planning a rendezvous by the end of the month, they vowed to check out possibilities.

Not all Germans appreciated the U.S. military occupation in their country. Only the older inhabitants, who could remember the death and destruction, sought the protection that the U.S. provided. Remnants of some bombed buildings remained to remind you of the grim devastation. Most of the younger masses were not happy with American Armed Forces in their country. It had been over twenty years since the war ended and they wanted our peaceful soldiers out of their nation. Needless to say, it was not the most hospitable situation for the American military living there. Trying not to take it personally, the guys were somewhat uncomfortable with the bitterness.

It didn't take long for hotel management to figure out we were ignoring employee policies and leaving allocated work stations. We were being reprimanded on a regular basis by these Germans, who were relentless about their work. They couldn't even take a joke! Justifying my anger, I compared their treatment to what our military friends described as passive resentment toward the Americans. Having another excuse for a pity party, I suppose we did deserve the scolding.

Meri tried to change the subject and stop our whining. She started mapping out the day trip to Heidelberg we had planned. Looking forward to exploring this famous city, founded early in the twelfth century, it had one of the oldest universities in the country. Heidelberg was most famous for its medieval fortress. My mood drastically improved as we talked about the upcoming outing. As long as we had a leisure-time activity to look forward to, the constant harassment was tolerable.

Waking up early to down a quick breakfast, two military guys picked us up near the airport. Paul and Andy had the day off and they asked to join our stopover of the castle tour in the Neckar Valley. While visiting this historic village, we discovered the Holy Ghost Church and learned that for over two-hundred years both Lutheran and Catholic services were held in the same hall. Ending the afternoon at the university, we observed a student demonstration. From what I could tell, the ungrateful scholars were protesting the high cost of ticket prices for riding local street cars to and from their classes. We watched these objectors in disgust. Their opposition seemed silly and trivial compared to the solemn Vietnam War protests and race riots we left behind in our own country.

Shopping, eating, and taking pictures were always part of being tourists. The weather was very drizzly, so we spent more time inside little shops looking at the hand-carved wooden clocks, the crystal glassware, porcelain figurines, and leather handbags. The guys offered to pay for dinner and drinks at the infamous Red Ox student inn. After a few hours, we drove back to Frankfurt. Trying not to be rude, we invited Paul and Andy up to our "den of sin," even though it was against the rules. They stayed for a short while before heading back to their lonely G.I. bunks.

We took it upon ourselves to go downtown to the employment office to pick up our work permits and passports. Hotel staff usually took care of this provision, but Meri was concerned we wouldn't have our credentials in time for traveling. Lenny and Gary (Sam had to work) wanted to go to Berlin the first of July and we needed to be prepared. Besides, not having passports was rather unsettling in such a somber environment.

Most of the populace followed the codes and standards with unyielding obligation. Amazingly, we had no hassles with the department of employee relations.

I was counting the days until we could leave the labor camp. To gain more control of our daily actions, the hausdame scheduled us to work the evening shift indefinitely.

Overeating was my outlet for dealing with frustrations, and my clothes were getting tighter by the day. When you're a petite, short girl, a few extra pounds make a huge difference. Our military friends weren't helping my waistline either. With late-night dinners, midnight snacks, and too many hamburgers and fries on the run, my body would never be the same. Working the night shift was causing havoc with regular sleeping. Staying out late, sometimes until four in the morning, and sleeping until noon, was unbecoming. Longing for a more normal existence, I felt like my life was out of control.

The guys were taking us out to parties at some dubious places. The Hut, a wild and extreme nightclub scene, was supposedly featured in *Playboy* magazine. Racially mixed couples paired up together. You didn't see blacks and whites pairing to dance together where I was raised. But then again, the "Baptist Bible Belt" had very few ethnic groups in residency period. At one time, black people were not even allowed on the public square after sunset. Times had changed!

Admittedly, I was drinking more alcoholic beverages. With no legal drinking age there, many well-meaning men bought our cocktails everywhere we went. Drinking sweet wine during dinner, apricot brandy after dinner, and mixed drinks late in the evening became the norm. Not only was I getting fat, I was turning into a lush. Ironically, on the way to the dorm one evening, after a late-night out, a runaway beer cart crashed into my legs just outside the service entrance at the hotel. I'm not sure who was more tipsy, me or the cart. My shins were black and blue with bruises.

Despite my overeating and drinking, the accelerated life was exciting and the exposure to new surroundings and foreign people was stimulating. Visitors and workers were from every part of the world. An Australian guest gave me a bottle of wine and a man from Saudi Arabia presented fine chocolates. Discussions didn't always flow evenly, and pronunciations were never easy to understand, but everyone tried hard to relate. The commonality we sought with one another was about making meaningful connections, if only for an evening, an hour, or just for the moment. Although I couldn't buy expensive souvenirs, I would take back a great deal more. Growing in knowledge and awareness was worth more than any material thing. Becoming more aware of the differences between the people and their cultures was invaluable. Eager to fill up my uninformed head, I listened as much as possible. The dissimilar viewpoints from these foreigners were enlightening. They had so much to offer in opening up my heart to tolerance and diversity.

On the other hand, there were those guys who wanted more than just casual conversation. It could be exasperating! Meri and I planned to return to the States, complete college, and acquire a marketable skill. Melody was emotionally confused, but in a potential long-term relationship. Not looking for involvement with any aggressive suitor, as much as I desired company from the opposite sex, most of the attention was too much. Claudio aspired to marry me so he could move to the United States. Chris and Bruno would stop over late evenings and occasionally fall asleep. The extreme undersized apartment was hardly big enough for three people let alone two overnight guests. Sometimes Lenny would drop by early with breakfast on his way to the base. They meant well, but it was hard to get sufficient rest with the constant invasion of our privacy. I was a mess!

Wiesbaden was next on our lists of places to review. This ancient city on the Rhine River was founded in the third-century BC and was once a Roman spa town. The popular thermal springs are still used today. Leaving early one warm and muggy morning, we encountered no drivers who dared to stop and offer to share a ride. Knowing quite well it was against the law to auto-stop on the autobahn, we walked toward the entry of the highway just as a patrolling policeman blinked his lights, waving us over.

Cringing at the sounds of those German police car sirens from the Nazi era, the officer was not amused by our trespassing on the freeway, nor was he very forgiving. He demanded our passports, and in order to get them back, we had to accompany him to the station and pay the fine of twenty-five deutsch marks. Not only did we get flashed by the bright red lights of the law enforcement car, we had to ride behind bars in the backseat of the automobile. Guilty as charged, I handed over my five dollars for the ticket and was more than humiliated. As resident lawbreakers in a foreign country, we now had criminal records on file. Melody was chuckling, but I couldn't see the humor. I'd never been arrested in my life. I was mortified!

Eventually we made it to Wiesbaden, just in time for the rain. Taking a bus tour was the only option. Volkswagen cars and vans drove alongside the coach in the jam-packed, automobile-choked streets. The air was filled with strains of Bach and Beethoven. The buildings looked as if they popped out of a *Hansel and Gretel* fairy tale book. Colorful flower boxes lined the front windows of the brightly painted houses. Driving through town, I watched the pedestrians as they walked in the public market places. Farmers set up vending stalls with their wares. Every table was covered with a large circular, striped umbrella to protect goods from spring showers. Millie, one of the maids, recommended taking the boat ride back to Frankfurt along the Rhine River. On the cruiser we saw castle after castle perched high along the mountains over the water. The scenery was worth every penny and the water was clear and smooth as glass. As the evening evolved, I felt as if I were going back in time, to the medieval era. Included in the ticket price was foodstuff. An assortment of dried fruits, fresh garden vegetables, sliced breads, and fat sausages were served on a colossal platter.

While eating, I overheard someone talking about Judy Garland. She died that day in England. Having seen *The Wizard of Oz* so many times as a child, I could recite most of the movie lines by memory. It was probably one of the best motion pictures ever made. Sitting there in mourning, I could almost hear Dorothy singing "Somewhere Over the Rainbow." And we for sure weren't in Kansas! A live performance of singers and dancers began to entertain the passengers as the waiters served beer. One of Germany's oldest and best-known customs is the consumption of beer. They drank the warm refreshments with zeal and gusto. Every variety of beer, whether dark or light, sweet or bitter, weak or strong, top- or bottom-fermented, was offered. Although the beverage tasted bitter, I drank a few sips. Developing a taste for beer was not important; I preferred a sweeter drink. The waiter brought me a glass of Riesling wine, thank you, very much! Not every person in Germany drinks beer. Thinking about Mark, I raised my glass in a toast. *Guten Trinken*!

A band played familiar German songs using the traditional musical instruments. An accordion, drum, trumpet, and trombone players showed off with vivacious and catchy tunes. Stuffing on the food and wine, we laughed and sang the "ohm-pa-pa" over and over again. As the sun set and the night lights grew brighter, the views became more captivating. Sitting in a stupor from the wine, holding myself in the cool nighttime air, I was glad I remembered to bring my overcoat. As expected, we got in quite late after the four-hour boat ride and the walk back to the hotel in the rain.

Melody woke up ailing. She wasn't sure if it was something she ate or an inflamed appendix. After calling Gary at the air base, he rushed right over and drove her to the medical clinic. Luckily, through our friendly connections, she was examined by an American physician and released in good health.

I was convinced that the greasy, high-fat "kraut" food was causing Mel's stomach ailments. In America, healthy eating was a national concern. In Germany, however, dining out on pig was the national pastime, which they called "Gut Essen Geben." Pork was their most popular protein dish. We'd been consuming too many frankfurters in this town that invented the hot dog. Bread had been the basic food of the German people for centuries, but the potato, "*die kartoffel,*" is the king of the German vegetables. No wonder we were getting sick and gaining weight! Gorging on the high-carbohydrate diet for almost a month was not good for anyone, let alone "little women."

With the end of the month quickly approaching, I started my farewells to fellow workers who knew we'd be leaving in a few days. Many of our friends came by to wish us well and give some meaningful mementos. Melford, one of the more cordial German employees, wanted to buy us dinner at the fairground. A summer carnival attracted crowds with thrill rides, games, and cotton candy. Playing a ring toss, I won a Bavarian mug to use for drinking my wine. Thrilled at winning this competition, I received an authentic blue and tan beer stein. Painted on the glass were two deer, a dog, and a hunter, in a woodsy background. This treasured prize became my personal keepsake.

Melody was feeling better so we squeezed in a side trip to a small town called Rudesheim. The adorable village was delightful, with many decorated shops and restaurants. The natives wore time-honored costumes, men in lederhosen, and women in pleated folksy dresses. Bands played and we danced the polka in the streets. Tourists trap towns were fun, as long as you joined in the carousing. Celebrating Christmas in June, we walked the pebble-stoned streets while listening to the Siegfried mechanical music sounds. After all, Saint Nicholas is synonymous with Germany.

Despite the fattening food and tough working conditions, I was enamored by the mountains and gorgeous countryside. Trying to think more positively, I wanted to have special memories of Deutschland. Melody and I rode a gondola to the top of one of the hillsides. Watching the flowing river and enchanting castles below gave me a chance to create a cherished memory.

* * *

The last day of the month arrived and paychecks were handed out. Opening up the envelopes in the privacy of our room, I could scarcely believe the amount. There had to be some mistake! For the hard work we did over four weeks' time, the total came to about fifty American dollars. There were numerous deductions to explain the diminutive compensation. Money was subtracted for the room, meals, uniform rental, country and city taxes, a church fee, and a fine for prematurely breaking a three-month contract. Not surprisingly, we weren't the first workers leaving early!

Management had room checks from time to time, and they could figure out our exit strategy. The reward package was exactly half of what we expected to be paid, and I didn't even like their food.

We counted on that money for traveling, but now we would have to come up with a different plan. There was no way we could afford to buy train tickets to Berlin. Melford warned us several times that our hitchhiking into East Germany was not safe. My thoughts were raging, and to think, I'd even felt guilty about not giving any prior notice. Melody said we deserved better and Meri was speechless. Touting the inequity, I didn't care anymore what they thought of my contempt. I was quite sure American employers would not have treated foreign students this way. They obviously didn't like our arrogance and we got what they thought was fair. They were the Gestapo!

Venting was loud, and harsh words were flying around the room as we did last-minute packing. I couldn't stop thinking about the injustice. All those beds we made day after day, over and over again. Then on evening shift, we went back into those same rooms and turned down the covers on those same beds, over and over again. I never wanted to make another bed the rest of my entire life!

Maybe we did bend the rules some, but we weren't from their country. They could have been a little more understanding and tolerant. After all, we were just temporary guest workers. Trying hard to shut off my racing mind, I had to get some sleep. In a few short hours, before the sun was up, we would slip out the back stairs, never to return again. While praying for easy rides and safe travels, I drifted off into a distraught slumber.

East Berlin border

CHAPTER 4

—

TUESDAY, JULY 1

A new month and a new day dawned. We were off on another adventure and eventually to a new job. The guys picked us up early and we traveled part-way on the train to save on expenses. Arriving in Hannover, we split up to hitchhike on to West Berlin. Getting rides was effortless and we met the guys at the East German border. However, unbeknownst to them, our military friends were not allowed through security gates, even in civilian clothes. The free city of West Berlin was surrounded by the Soviet-occupied East Germany. They decided to return to Hannover, catch a flight into West Berlin, and meet us at the Brandenburg Gate on Wednesday.

A German businessman named Erwin Gudladt offered our transportation through East Germany. Settling into his roomy luxury car, I started to listen to the radio announcements. Earlier in the afternoon, Queen Elizabeth named her twenty-year-old son Charles the Prince of Wales. Thinking back on my childhood, I remembered my mom used to tell me to grow up and marry this Prince Charles. We'd go to Great Britain by the end of the summer and I started fantasizing about meeting him.

Traveling through this inter-zonal territory involved stopping at numerous checkpoints. The uniformed guards watched on the ground and in towers while holding handguns and rifles. High fences lined both sides of the highway. This was not a movie set and I was awfully grateful to be with this man who knew the protocol of crossing the heavily secured area. The East German roads were all but empty. Few cars traveled the bleak and barren highways. Intermittently we passed a giant billboard with communist slogans and pictures of communist heroes plastered over it. Few countries bear such an ugly, tortured history and it was still evident from what I observed. Since 1945, the Iron Curtain cut across Germany. For more than five-hundred and sixty miles, walls, minefields, and barbed wire entanglements blocked the routes that traverse the heart of Germany. After several hours, we finally arrived in West Berlin. Erwin not only bought our dinner, he drove us to a secure hotel. Showing a concerned interest in our safety, he left his phone number and address, in case we needed further assistance. Mr. Gudladt was our knight in a shiny black Mercedes. Melody was sure we'd never have made it safely if it were not for his help. I, on the other hand, wondered why Lenny and Gary suggested going to East Berlin in the first place.

The following morning we took a bus to the Brandenburg Gate. The city of Berlin was almost destroyed during the war. In the rebuilt city, residuals of destruction still existed. A half-bombed building, the shattered Kaiser Wilhelm Memorial Church, was within sight. Serving as a constant reminder of the remnants and devastation, West Berlin was like an island behind a metal screen. The city-state is the capital of the Federal Republic of Germany and since August 1961, Berlin had been divided by the wall. Waiting near the closely fortified gate until noon, the guys never showed up. Having no idea where they were, and being naturally worried, we had no choice but to go on without them.

In order to survey the other side, it was compulsory to leave our passports at the guarded hut. As the sightseeing bus drove from one side of the gate to the other, the surroundings quickly changed from color to black and white. In the dreary existence, people wore drab clothing and worn-out shoes. There was no sense of urgency, no hustle, no bustle, no passion in their steps. Many were dressed in their armies' uniforms, as they marched stiff and joyless. Hearing no laughter or crying in the streets, Meri commented on how demoralizing their lives seemed. It was heartbreaking. Intently thinking about my own freedoms, for the first time in earnest, I fully understood and appreciated my liberated country and what freedom really means. *God bless us and them*, I uttered to myself. The tour guide spoke English and informed the riders of the shrines we drove past. There was the Russian Monument, the Soviet Embassy, Humboldt University, the House of Soviet Culture, and Marx-Engels Square. Continuing on around Alexander Square to Lenin and Stalin Avenues, the drive concluded at the Soviet War Memorial in their solemn Garden of Remembrance. These tributes were meant to impress the tourists but they seemed rather deceiving. It was blatantly obvious that their government's showy prosperity didn't touch the citizens or their unfulfilled lives.

After completing the tour, I fretted until my passport was back in my possession. What a relief to be on the free side of the wall! The tour left me feeling stunned and bewildered. Melody said we needed to go shopping. Most of our buying consisted of small items, as money was never in abundance. Besides, we didn't want to carry a bunch of packages while on foot around town. I bought one remembrance gift and a postcard to send home. Every day while traveling, I sent messages to my family, letting them know where we were and where we were headed. However, by the time the cards arrived back in Missouri, we were long gone from most places.

While looking through the rack of postcards, I came across a card with a picture of former President John F. Kennedy. On the card was the quote *"Ich bin ein Berliner."* He shouted this during a goodwill visit to Berlin in the early sixties. Gazing at his photo brought back gloomy memories of that dreadful day just five years earlier in Dallas, as parade bystanders watched his fatal shooting. Everyone remembered exactly where they were when he was killed. His brutal assassination shocked the whole world, and he must have been loved by many in Berlin.

Strolling through the west side of Berlin, we came across Schoenberg Town Hall, where the freedom bell rings daily. What a wonderful sound along with the street and traffic noises and the people talking and walking about freely. Everything was business as usual, despite close boundary lines that divided the free city, from the gated communist city. Freedom is priceless!

We found an old hotel in the downtown section that was inexpensive and clean. Walking up the double-wide staircase to the room, I opened the doors to a suite filled with huge, old-fashioned furniture. The bedding was made of fancy white linen covers spread over fluffy feather-stuffed mattresses. High ceilings and wood-carved wall panels presented an affluent appearance. As Melody flung herself on the bed, she looked like a princess in waiting. It was fun pretending!

We freshened up before going out and found a local discotheque to listen to some dance tunes. After a few glasses of wine, the midnight hour advanced, so we hastened back to the hotel. None of us read the hours of operation and didn't notice the doors locked at eleven o'clock. Not knowing what else to do, I started pounding on the wood frame so hard that my hands were hurting. Exasperated and distraught, we flopped down on the steps and tried to get some rest. In the early morning hours, a man who worked at the hotel came along and unlocked the door. Collapsing in our clothes on top of the full-sized antique beds, I drifted off to sleep without setting the alarm.

Closer to noontime, before we got up and around, we departed Berlin down Kurfuerstendamm Strasse or Kudamm Street. Having difficulty getting anyone to stop in the afternoon, eventually an older gentleman took us out of the city. Arthur Dietz promised to send everyone Christmas cards, as we exchanged addresses. Thirty minutes later two young men from Turkey stopped in a tattered car. The auto was having obvious problems and they drove at a snail's pace. What should have only been a three-hour trip turned into five hours. Twilight loomed as we dragged into Nuremberg. Going directly to an American military hotel, even though it was only for enlisted personnel and their families, due to the late hour, we talked the desk clerk into renting out a room for one night.

While getting ready for bed, I thought about my dad, who was stationed in Germany nearly twenty-five years earlier. He was quite young during the war, about my age, roaming this country under violent circumstances. Spending time in Augsburg, just south of where we were staying, he served in the United States Army Air Corps and had a certain affinity for this country. After all those years, it was a shame our military were still keeping watch where the Cold War continued.

Nuremberg, a well-known city in Germany, was once the location of the annual congress of the Nazi Party. After the war, the trials of the Nazi war criminals were also held in this city. In earlier times, trader routes for ginger, cloves, and saffron spices passed through the village. Sweet spicy honey cakes were produced for revenue and consumption. Also a center for learning and art, the small settlement was built around a castle in the eleventh century. In modern times, there are still beekeeping districts scattered in the wooded forests around the community. Stopping for a bite to eat, we tried some of the syrupy spiced cakes that are as much a part of Nuremberg as were Adolph Hitler's rules for the "nordic race" and his horrific racial laws against the Jews.

Reading from the guide book, Meri let us know the Christmas fair was one of the best. During the holiday season, old town streets would be crammed with people, for the *Christkindlmarkt* (Christ Child Market). Shiny bells and balls, angels, and stars would adorn the Christmas trees. In an age of plastic and metal playthings, the children still loved the wooden toys from Nuremberg. Woodcarving was an established craft in most German-speaking countries. Melody found a kids toy store to explore and we watched tiny jumping jacks dancing on their strings. There were precious wooden dolls, coo-coo clocks, and the many animals from Noah's Ark. Carefully inspecting each price tag, I ended up buying a small, carved, wooden man. Only two inches high with rosy red cheeks, he wore a black top-hat on his jumbo-sized head. His full, happy smile reminded me of the fun times I spent while traveling through this complex country.

Heading out of town, we stumbled into a very impressive Lutheran church. St. Lorenzkirche was built in 1439 and not completed for forty more years. Stained-glass windows filled the side walls. Biblical themes and the lives of various saints were displayed through pictorial stories. Beautiful reds, oranges, blues, and greens on white glass with heavy black lead outlines, formed the awe-inspired drawings. Every single church we stumbled upon had its own unique style and character.

Picking up a pamphlet as we left the church, I read about the invention of the printing press. In the mid-fifteenth century, German-born Johannes Gutenberg mass-produced copies of books while using movable type. Since he published the first Bible, the book was named for him. Another interesting Nuremberg native, Albrecht Durer, inscribed and illustrated the first book written by one artist.

As much as I wanted to keep looking around this interesting, historic township, Frankfurt was beckoning. We couldn't procrastinate any longer and had to get back to make final arrangement for storing all the extra baggage, gifts, and souvenirs. A jolly, portly truck driver from Holland hauled us back to our former place of employment.

Against my better judgment, we went by the airport hotel to visit some former friends and co-workers. Chris and Bruno were able to get away from the labor camp and fill us in on the latest gossip. Melody called the air base and Lenny and Gary came right over. Anxiously waiting to find out what in the world happened to them on the trip, it seems they missed their flight in Hannover and had no way to convey any message. Everything happens for a reason!

Gary picked up our stored suitcases at the Frankfurt train station, offering to ship our gifts and parcels back to Missouri courtesy of the United States Military. Regrettably, I trusted Lenny to send my rolls of undeveloped film to my family. I thought it might be a reprieve for them to see photographs, but the package was lost in the mail. I was sick about the missing pictures that no one ever got to see.

Going with the guys to the base, we attended a celebration for the fourth of July. After the street party and watching the late-night fireworks display, we ended up spending the night in their off-base housing unit. The last night in Germany we spent cleaning up the apartment of the same guys who offered us a place to live only a few weeks prior. I never thought I would actually be picking up after them. One favor deserves another, and they did help us out on many occasions.

Putting off the inevitable, it was time to say good-bye to our favorite guys. Promising to write one another, Lenny and I talked about meeting in New York someday. As much as I believed we would see each other again, distance separates and things change. For a very short time, we were bosom buddies, during that month of June 1969. I would never forget him!

Despite the trials and tribulations we had while working at the hotel, there were innumerable extraordinary times with the people we met. One of the officers at the base offered assistance and a ride to the German border town of Basel. He was from Kansas City and went to the same high school Meri attended. Leaving Germany was not easy! It took forever to get through the passport inspections and customs lines as the stern uniformed guards checked everything twice. Finally, we were allowed to pass security and cross the border. Fierce German Shepherd police dogs barked loudly from behind. I was nervous and Melody didn't dare make any snide remarks.

Leaving beautiful Germany, we crossed in to an even more beautiful, mountainous country. Switzerland is surrounded by giant nations on all sides. Driving past Swiss-German villages situated between rolling hills, jade green meadows, and pointed snow-covered mountain tops, we drove on to Interlaken. This quaint tourists' town was where we would live and work through the month of July. The views were absolutely divine. An alluring lake was on one side of the town, and the Swiss Alps were on the far side. I could hardly contain my ecstasy, as I looked at the stunning emerald-green surroundings. Working in this wealthy industrialized country was going to be absolutely fabulous!

Daylight disappeared by the time we arrived at Hotel Krone, resembling a bed and breakfast compared to the contemporary hotel we were used to working. The smaller building was older, family-owned and -operated, with only twenty-five rooms. Presenting my letter to the desk clerk, he called to the hotel owner in the back room. He proceeded to tell us the guests included young British school-aged kids staying a week at a time for the summer holidays. This certainly sounded like something we could handle. Looking over at Meri and Melody, I flashed a big grin their way.

Mrs. Mooser, the owner, spoke little English, but she received my signed letter of acceptance. She needed English-speaking workers to clean the rooms and serve breakfasts and dinners to the youngsters. Confirmation letters for reservations would also have to be sent out to the guests. With only two available job positions, Frau Mooser offered to contact another local hotel owner who might have an opening. She would call first thing in the morning about possible employment.

We followed her older daughter, who spoke a little English, up the stairs to employee rooms. In the attic of this four-story structure were two bedrooms looking much like "Pollyanna" accommodations. In the unfinished corner of the A-framed room was a small window with a great view of snow-covered Jungfrau Mountain. At the end of the narrow, uneven hallway, was the only bathroom. Unfortunately, there was no hot water. Shivering at the thought of bathing and washing my hair in cold water, I couldn't think of any worse torture. Not a big fan of outdoor camping, I grimaced in agony at the thought of cleaning my face and body in freezing water.

Tired and cranky from the long travel day, it didn't take long to sponge-bathe. In the small but cozy quarters with only two single beds, Meri and I agreed to double up together. We were asked to report to work the next day with employee breakfasts served at seven o'clock. After writing letters home, disclosing new jobs and addresses, I turned out the lights. Trying not to roll over on Meri, I couldn't seem to get situated. The next thing I heard was the sound of the ringing alarm.

* * *

After finishing eggs, toast, and fruit, on a table in the basement kitchen, we rushed off to the second-floor dining room. Hurriedly serving breakfasts to a dozen or so loud middle school boys, the first day was testy. Hungry kids could be vicious! After wiping off tables, making beds, and straightening up the bathrooms, we were free for a few hours. Working a split-shift would be necessary, as we had to return promptly at five o'clock to serve dinners to the starving brood.

Repulsive uniforms were not mandatory but we were expected to keep the boy's rooms squeaky clean. Switzerland strives to be a dirt-free country. Shop owners were out each morning, literally sweeping the streets with brooms. They seemed to be an extremely hard working bunch of folks. Betty and Margaret, the other Swiss maids, provided meticulous instructions for proper scouring techniques. Housekeeping was serious business in these hospitality hotels!

The Hotel Krone would be a better place to live and work. The staff was friendly, the guests were youngsters, and the food was mouth-watering. Hot, buttered, homemade bread with every meal. Food, glorious food—the great comforter and remedy for whatever ails you. Trying to eat less was going to be difficult. It seemed everything we did centered on eating. I would put off my dieting for another month. For the love of food!

CHAPTER 5

—

SUNDAY, JULY 7

Frau Moser, secured another position with room and board at a hotel seven miles away in a little town called Oberried. Melody volunteered to take this job offer. We would visit each other on off days and with the swing shifts, we could always go over between serving meals. Melody seemed okay with the separation. I think she needed some time alone.

After lunch, we were free to go but had to return at four to get ready for the dinner hour. Meri was ready to venture out and see the town. Interlaken, a popular tourist area, offered many kinds of recreational sports, such as hiking, biking, camping, and boating. Souvenir shops jam-packed the streets as visitors came from the world over. The highest cogwheel railway station in Europe offered a train ride for brave souls to the top of Jungfrau Mountain at a height of 13,648 feet.

The rain kept the lush grass watered but kept Meri and me inside the second day in Interlaken. Hanging out in the bedroom arranging our things, we discussed school and friends. For the first time since leaving home, I was homesick. A phone call from Europe would be way too expensive and I didn't dare make any calls back home. My father gave me strict orders to call only in case of an emergency. Homesickness would most certainly not qualify as an urgent condition. Sitting there in my reflective mood, I wondered if any of my good friends were thinking of me.

Meri and I were up every morning by six, getting dressed and ready to clean guest's rooms. Sheets and linens had to be ironed by hand before making the beds. One morning we were sent to sweep a filthy closet storeroom, and carry heavy boxes up from the wine cellar. Feeling like Cinderella before the prince arrived, most mornings my feet hurt so badly I could hardly walk. Swollen and sore from standing all day, my legs felt that the work was definitely harder and the hours longer. The calmer environment was less stressful and more acceptable. Even though I was completely worn to a frazzle by the end of each ten-hour day, I was more content in my new surroundings.

Swiss people take great pride in serving their guests and tourists with the best of everything. The food was more appetizing, beef instead of pork, more fruits and vegetables as well as dairy and egg products. As much as I needed to lose a few pounds, it would be hard to resist the healthy meals. Every day we were served the same feasts the cook fixed for the students and that also included any leftovers we wanted to take back for snacking.

On days we finished work early, Meri and I would hitch a ride over to make a visit with Melody. Interlaken is located between two vast lakes; to the west is Lake Thun and Lake Brienz is to the northeast. The village of Oberried was on the north shore of Lake Brienz. While taking a walk by the Tannhorn Mountain, along the pathway we came across some edelweiss, the national flower of Switzerland.

Melody worked in a charming alpine chalet with breathtaking scenery in every direction. The gingerbread town was full of multicolored houses adorned with the usual window flower boxes. Sitting on the dock dangling our tender feet in the lake, we discussed the new work situations. Melody was satisfied. She also appreciated the less structured labor conditions and didn't mind the added work load. Her employer treated her like family and provided a comfortable sleeping room.

Later that same evening, Meri and I went to another hotel to check out some dancing availability. Native folklore and modern rock 'n' roll were alive and well in the Victoria Jungfrau Grand Hotel. A live band played and there were plenty of guys to pick for dancing partners. I enjoyed watching others dance as much as I loved to dance. Not only did it provide a great way to meet people, I was also burning calories. Two Italians, Raffaele and Carmelo, joined our table. Slow dancing to a sensuous song called "Je t'aime" gave me a chance to rest my winded lungs and worn out legs.

Switzerland has as many people as it has valleys. The native countrymen speak three different languages. Although the majority of the population speaks German, French and Italian are spoken in the border towns. Their culture is quite varied, from the rugged hardy mountain people, to the cosmopolitan city dwellers. Many foreigners of different nationalities, often visited this normally unassuming country. No matter the time of day there was a mix of tourists on the streets, in the night clubs, or congregating in the hotel bars. Weekend nights could be a walker's rush hour.

Travel can be a great teacher and I learned as much from being immersed in the culture, as I learned from the many churches, monuments, and museums. Sociology was my first college major (as it was for most students during the sixties) labeling me a "people person." Meri was also interested in the social sciences and was pleased to be in this distinctive county. The well-known Swiss psychiatrist, Dr. Carl Jung, lived and worked in Zürich.

Included in the history of Switzerland, is their national hero, the legendary Wilhelm Tell, who shot an arrow through an apple off the head of his young son. His statue is in dozens of Swiss towns and every evening, the story was told through a play dramatization, in the town square. The fictitious Tell proved to be more alive than any other native. He was the kind of resilient man that most of the Swiss men aspired to be and his famous crossbow is the trademark of every exported product.

Some mornings would be damp, in the cool mountain air, and taking a bath and washing my hair in cold water proved to be a painful awakening. Getting ready for work was often agonizing! One cold morning, we spent too much time under the covers, which resulted in Meri and my receiving a reprimand for being late. Goosebumps covered my body as I commenced to clean. Ironing that day was a sheer pleasure, as the warmth of the hot iron on my cold hands, and wet hair, provided a welcomed heat.

Each week when a new group of kids arrived, we had the privilege of meeting them at the train station. Only one group of girls vacationed at the hotel during our tenure. Forty-two young men from Great Britain followed us to the hotel our first week. Ranging in ages from ten to fifteen, they spoke so fast we could hardly understand them. They were salivating! After serving those steaming hot dinners, to the distinguished Brits, we were free for the remainder of the evening.

Frau Mooser and her daughter proposed a visit to friends of theirs. At an adjacent hotel, they had wine and dessert. Joining them for the sweet indulgences, we ate in silence but smiled often. Finding it difficult to take part in the conversation, the Swiss German dialect was not like the German language I was used to hearing. Watching these people socialize with food and drink, was entertainment enough. Frau Mooser, a robust lady with big apple cheeks, moved exceedingly slow and laughed frequently. Her laughter was contagious as we ate, and drank, with these merry working-class people. They seemed genuinely focused on making our stay a pleasant experience.

The next morning was awfully busy with such an enormous group of boys to serve. Mrs. Ludy, a lovely middle-aged lady, managed the dining-room operations. In broken English, she patiently showed me how to get the food out of storage and ready to serve. Meri and I were awkward at times; thank goodness it was only kids we were serving. A dumb-waiter, from the basement kitchen appeared with the food, trays of fruit, eggs, sausages, and rolls. While scurrying from table to table, Meri dropped and broke a juice glass. Then, a full plate of rations slipped out of my hand, spilling food all over the floor. The teen boys snickered and hooted while clapping at our clumsy performances. Serving home-style allowed for talk, and teasing, during mealtimes.

After dinner, as the boys left the dining room, one of the young lads went tumbling down the stairs. He wasn't paying any attention to where he was walking and luckily the only thing that got hurt was his pride. Payback time! After we helped him up and made sure he was okay, Meri and I commenced to laugh with them. Roars of cheering and chuckles echoed up and down the halls.

Like one big happy family, the kids shared ridiculous stories while eating. I enjoyed listening to their adorable accents, as much as hearing the tales. Sometimes we'd fix box lunches for them to take on outings. Running into them in town, they would always stop to talk about their expedition. One night at a birthday bash for one of the kids, we ate cake and celebrated right along with them. When the groups left at the end of each week, saying good-bye was never easy. Some of the boys gave going-away gifts: small boxes of candy, souvenir bracelets, and hugs, lots and lots of hugs.

Meri and I went dancing at the Kursaal one evening, with the guys we met at the Victoria Hotel. Raffaele Loi and Carmelo Ciaramidaro were two of the many Italians working in the local hotels. They waited tables, learning the language, before going back to Italy to work. Even some of the live band members were really cute Italians with dark eyes, olive skin, and jet-black hair. Wearing silky satin shirts unbuttoned half-way down, they showed off their bare chests with gold necklaces. Wide lavender scarves, wrapped around their waists, accentuated the tight, tight, tight, crushed-velvet pants. Having so much fun, we lost track of time and when we got back to Hotel Krone, the doors were locked tight. Not again! This time, we didn't dare beat down the entrance.

Walking to the back of the building while scoping out the joint, I noticed that the dining-room window on the second floor was open. With no wire screens, we decided to scale up the side of the building to get inside. The guys helped me climb on top of some stacked fruit crates that were in the alley. As they held the rickety wood forms steady, Meri and I slid through the rolled out windows. Waving a silent good-bye, we tiptoed past the eating tables but still could not get out in to the hallway. The French door to the dining-room was latched, on the other side, and as hard as I jiggled, the lock would not jar open. Trying not to waken anyone, we tried to be quiet.

There was no way we could stay there all night. The predicament was grim as we both had to go to the restroom. Time was of an essence! Whispering to one another about what to do next, I looked around the room and spotted the dumb-waiter. One of us would have to ride the tiny box elevator to the basement. Meri weighed less by six or seven pounds so I helped her squeeze in. Barely fitting into the cabinet space designed for food and dishes, I nervously thought about what might happen if she were over the weight limit? Taking a deep breath, I gently pushed the down button, praying the cable wouldn't snap as she descended to the kitchen. Hail Mary, full of grace!

In a short time, Meri came back up the stairs, calmly letting me out of the locked room. Trying to hold back our laughter, we climbed the two more flights of stairs to the top story bedroom. As soon as I closed the loft passage door, we both started laughing so hard, I almost wet my pants.

After the "breaking and entering" incident, I told Meri we had to write a book someday. She agreed it would be a funny story. Meri was a good sport and I appreciated her willingness to help resolve the unexpected problems. Granted, we were learning to be resourceful through these trials. Dealing with some of the cultural differences was causing a few dilemmas. If we survived, the saga had to be told. Keeping a daily diary, every night I'd jot down a few notes about the many places we went and the people we met. Most of the journaling was an account of the day's events.

One day after lunch, taking a spur-of-the-moment trip with the kids, we caught a ride on the bus to Lucerne. Hopping off the van, with the teen boys as escorts, we crossed the fourteenth-century landmark bridge over the vividly blue, Lucerne Lake. A couple of the youngsters rented paddle boats so we floated the lake with them, enjoying the summer breeze while getting a workout.

Taking an excursion on a steamer-train cable car, it went straight up the side of Pilatus-Kulm Mountain. While ascending to the summit of the Bernese Alps, I watched the sparkling cobalt lake below, glistening in the sunlight. Riding back down the mountain at a shrill speed, when reaching the ground, we dashed off to hitch a ride back to the hotel. Not allowing enough time to get there by four, Mr. Mooser yelled at us in German. He was obviously angry with our tardiness!

Later on Raffaele and Carmelo showed up at the inn. They requested our company for late night spaghetti dinners. Questioning how we'd talk to our Italian friends, who could barely speak English, they actually wanted to practice our language. Over wine and pasta, we taught them correct grammar. Repeating the sentences several times, they tried hard to articulate the proper pronunciation. We learned these two were from the largest of the Italian islands, Raffaele was Sardinian and Carmelo was Sicilian. Not the least bit interested in learning any Italian, I found it hard enough to stay halfway proficient in German. However, I admired anyone who could speak more than one language. Learning from experience, I knew that it was no easy task.

The following afternoon, Meri and I rented motor scooters and headed to Lauterbrunnen. Considered to be one of the most spectacular glacial valleys, in all of Europe, we were ecstatic to be going on this ride. Manning a motorcycle was a bit shaky at first; I'd ridden as a passenger on cycles but never in the driver's seat. The adrenalin rush was invigorating as I timidly maneuvered the bike, up and down rolling hills, in the cool, mountain wind gusts. Yelling into the air currents helped me stay focused, as I tried to steer the cycle in the right direction. Far off in the distance, I could see the roaring cascade of gushing water, pouring down off the pictorial, Stabbach Waterfall.

Making a stop at a village wine festival, we parked the scooters and got off to take part in the tasting. The women were dressed in distinctive Swiss costumes. White pinafore aprons covered their printed skirts and puffy-sleeved blouses. The gentlemen wore short-shorts, knee high socks and green wool hats with stubby feathers poked on top. They danced and pranced in the streets to typical folk music. Clapping while watching, we sipped the wines, ate sweet biscuits, and listened to lively tunes played on accordions. When it came time to start my engine, miraculously, I lost my fear of steering the motor-scooter. Singing loudly in the wind, nothing else seemed to matter.

On Sunday mornings, after serving breakfasts to the guests, Meri and I would attend Mass at a small chapel near the hotel. Churches in Switzerland were not as complex as other European houses of adoration. John Calvin, spending most of his adult living in Geneva, broke away from the Roman Catholic Church during the Protestant Reformation. Understanding the need for useful religious reform, he disapproved of carved images and paintings of the saints. His puritanical faith persuasion was part of the extreme changes in the church. Calvinism was terribly restricting for the arts and no decorations, or colors, were allowed in the cathedrals for an extended time period.

If we didn't have to strip bed linens, there was usually time for a short Sunday outing. Catching a ride with a man from Czechoslovakia, he joined us a few hours in the small town of Grindelwald. This gorgeous mountain community is where skiing was first introduced to the Swiss by the English. However, in the warm summer months, mountaineering was the more popular activity for the athletic inclined.

Gillian, our loud obnoxious Czech driver, was keen on the current sports buzz. Inquiring if we knew Joe Namath had decided not to retire from pro-football after all, I nodded in ignorance at his newsworthy tip. Big deal! As far as I was concerned, football players were nothing more than modern day gladiators. Why a group of grown men, would brutally knock each other down, to claim a ball, was beyond my comprehension. But, I might watch the Swiss football players.

Meri, the official brochure interpreter, reported the resorts were once sanitariums used for sick tuberculin patients. They came to heal their infected lungs in the pure mountain air. These same convalescent homes were now the finest ski resorts in the Swiss Alps. Gazing out in the distance at the dynamic North Face of Eiger Peak and the Wetterhorn Mountain, they looked more like rocky cathedrals. Snow skiing was not an activity I had ever tried. With a trip planned to Winter Park, Colorado, over the Christmas break, I would get my chance to learn this graceful sport.

Stopping for ice cream, eager to try something new, I ordered a coffee flavored cone. As I hesitantly took my first lick, the sweet frozen treat was yummy, becoming a new favorite flavor. While walking along the sidewalk, licking my sugary delight, the smell of sweet flowers filled the air in the enchanting village. On every window ledge, whether homes or businesses, were wooden boxes full of colorful daisies, blue bells and an alpine assortment of posies. The peaceful walk ended and Gillian offered to drive us back to the hotel, just in time, for mess-hall duties.

Anxious to scout out other places for night life, we checked out the hotel bar. Most of the patrons were over thirty and we left the tavern as quickly as we entered. The casino was the more popular place for every age so we invited Paul and Walter to go along. They worked in the Hotel Krone kitchen and were game for spiffing-up and going out. Dress codes were strictly enforced at the fine clubs. Women had to wear skirts or dresses, and the men, sport coats and ties. If you didn't have a tie, you could borrow one from a basket full of ties at the entry-way. Watching the many gamblers was totally fascinating. While dressed in the latest and best contemporary fashions, they drank in the smoke filled rooms, tossing away their money, playing roulette and rolling dice.

Melody came over on Saturday night and we headed back to the fun casino. With no allotted change for the slots or games, at least we could sit in the lounge and listen to live entertainment. Most of the music was meant for the American tourists. Hearing songs by Johnny Cash and blues legend B.B. King, sung by these foreign singers, was a real treat. It didn't take long before someone would ask me to dance. Victor Black, a competent

Italian dancer, requested my hand as his "Twist" partner for a fast dance. Meri and Melody were also out on the floor, twisting the night away. One of the dancers, inadvertently, dumped his Coke on Meri as she finished a swirl. Time to go! Melody managed a ride back to Oberried with a guy she met from Holland.

Leaving the dance area, I had to enlighten my friends about a Roman romantic who told me he loved me. I'm quite sure it was the only English he knew. We'd just met on the dance floor that evening and he already loved me? I'd heard stories about these Italian Romeos, who could just "love 'em and leave 'em." Trying to maintain my innocence, I wasn't about to give up my old-school values with this stranger, regardless of how passionate he was. Besides, we couldn't even talk to each other. Not that he cared! Ignoring his impromptu statement, I had no interest in any after hour pillow talk. Besides, I was committed to saving myself for my future husband. Not every American girl was into "free love" as most of these foreigners liked to believe.

While walking down the hallway, we could hear a television in one of the casino game rooms. Tuned to the world news broadcasts, one of the journalists reported that Senator Edward Kennedy, from Massachusetts, drove off a bridge, plunging into the bay near Chappaquiddick Island. He survived the accident but his twenty-eight-year-old companion, Mary Jo Kopechne, was killed. The famed Kennedy family was continually making the headlines, and now another tragedy. As we stood in silent remorse, I repeated a little prayer I had learned in my early parochial school days. Cars were a good means of transportation but they were also machines that could kill. Making an earnest plea, for safer travels, we sure could use any extra assistance from our guardian angels.

Interlaken, Switzerland

CHAPTER 6

—

SUNDAY, JULY 20

Another Sunday rolled around and an overnight trip to the Greater Geneva was in the works. Several rides and several hours went by. Hitchhiking didn't always go well! Sooner, if not later, we'd get to the targeted city. Swiss landscape is probably the most spectacular and diverse in the entire world. Stunning mountains captivated our vision in every direction during the many miles of driving.

While gazing out the car window, intently listening to the radio broadcaster, the announcer blurted out a historic event to the entire world. On July twentieth, the United States landed the first men on the moon. Everyone was talking about the trip and I was so proud of our guys. Buzz Aldrin and Neil Armstrong, off the good ship Apollo 11, walked about the lunar surface for over two hours, while pilot Michael Collins orbited above. More than 600 million people watched television that day, as the two astronauts collected moon rocks. What an incredible trip!

Reminded again of President Kennedy, he believed we would land a man on the moon before the end of the decade. In 1961, to a joint session of congress, J.F.K. delivered a rallying speech. He expressed his belief that our nation should commit to achieving this goal, not because it would be easy, but because it would be hard. This challenge, that he wanted our country to accept and not postpone, would be one we would win. His vision had been accomplished and he was no longer alive to see what our nation did with their best talents, energies and skills. All of mankind was impressed and maybe John Kennedy was watching, from a far better place than the rest of us.

We stopped in Montreux to see the famous thirteenth-century Chateau de Chillon, located on the eastern shores of Lake Geneva. The twenty-five separate villas and gardens were gradually connected to form a stronghold. This impressive thousand years old castle was graced by gorgeous, lakefront footage. Lord Byron wrote the poem "The Prisoner of Chillon" making the castle popular in the 1800s. This imprisonment was the true story of a Genovois monk, Francois Bonivard. In the near distance, we could hear music in the air, coming from the Jazz Festival in Geneva.

After finding a place to spend the night, we went searching for a church. Sunday Mass was as much a part of my weekend routine as shopping. Meri didn't seem to mind the ritual in her timetable. I think she enjoyed seeing the splendid European cathedrals. The closest place we could find for evening service was Holy Trinity Anglican Church on Rue du Mont Blanc. Meri was delighted to hear French spoken, in this global city, occupied by French speaking Swiss.

When Mass ended, taking advantage of the additional daylight, we took in a few more sites. Mount Blanc, the highest mountain in Europe, could be seen from Lac Leman (French, for Lake Geneva). Where the lake empties into the Rhone River was the highest artificial fountain, in the world, the Jet d'Eau. Watching this incredible spray of water, spurt over four-hundred feet up, was amazing. Two French guys, walking near the lake, invited us to join them for dinner.

Morning began with an extended tour of the European Headquarters of the United Nations. Switzerland was prevented from joining the UN due to the organizations system of collective security. The Swiss have joined many relief groups and the Red Cross was founded, in Geneva, during the mid-1800s. Who doesn't recognize the familiar flag, a red cross against a white background? Since 1945, the League of Red Cross societies, distributed tons of food and medical supplies, to peoples displaced by revolutions and wars. Impressed, after learning about this generous philanthropy, I also knew the United States was very bighearted when it came to helping the needy. I promised myself to go back home and donate blood once in awhile.

Principles of neutrality are cherished by the Swiss people. History records that in 1481 a hermit, known as Nicholas of Flue was able to persuade fighting Swiss confederates to settle differences by compromise, rather than by fighting. He is credited with fathering the neutrality commitment that has managed to keep Switzerland out of most wars. But like scores of other countries, their native soil has had their fair share of religious wars between the Protestants and the Catholics.

The Swiss also like to brag that they are members of the League of Nations. And last but not least, one of the very first English-language Bibles was published in Geneva in the mid-1500s. My brain was over-stuffed with information and I was in need of a well-deserved shopping break.

After buying a Swiss watch and admiring my new purchase, I noticed it was getting late and we needed to get back to work. A gregarious Swiss student offered a ride and we talked about the newly acquired information we learned while it was still fresh on our minds. He mentioned the famous eighteenth-century philosopher, Jean Jacques Rousseau, who was also from Geneva. Dropping Meri and I off, at the entrance of the hotel, we waved good-bye to Paul as he sped on down the road.

Meri gasped franticly, realizing she'd forgotten her purse in his car. It wasn't long before Paul circled back and returned the billfold. His honesty said much about his character and moral fiber. Meri gave him a great big hug and a kiss. Once again, my opinion about this country was reinforced. These practical, hard working, people showed outstanding hospitality to their numerous guests. Although I was a foreign worker, I liked to think of myself as a guest.

After the kids were well fed, we still had enough energy to go out the remainder of the night. We both wanted to try out the Swiss cheese and chocolate fondues, at the local bistro. Even though chocolate making was first introduced by the Italians, it was later adapted to machine production, by the Swiss. Their very best-known milk chocolate producer is "the very best," the Nestle Company. The waiter noted there were thirty-six chocolate factories in Switzerland. Naturally we had to order several varieties. Meri was a true chocoholic; she ate chocolate almost every day.

Receiving a long letter from home, I relished hearing from family and friends. My mom was terrific about writing humorous, detailed messages. Every week she kept me posted on what was going on with my many brothers and other relations. My dad would send money, which I'd promptly spend on presents for the relatives. Gifts from other countries had special meaning. Wishing to buy more, my family was too big and my resources too limited for very much.

On many afternoons, Meri and I would go visit nearby towns, around the lakes, in the beautiful mountain playground. We wanted to take a glimpse of everything this great valley had to offer. The Castle of Schadau located in the city of Thun, near the River Aare, stands in an English style park. On the north shore of Lake Thun is the Castle of Oberhofen, dating back to the middle ages. High above Lake Thun is the village of Beatenberg with St. Beatus Cave which was once the home of a dragon. Located on the south bank of Lake Thun is Spiez, another gorgeous settlement with a medieval castle and stunning views of the lake and mountains. And on the north bank of Lake Brienz, the city with the same name flaunts the thundering, and breathtakingly beautiful, Giessbach waterfalls.

Backpackers and climbers traipsed over the grand Alps, which make up sixty percent of the country. Minuscule towns were built in the sides of the mountains. In the summer months, the rural dairy farmers herded their belled cattle from the village barns and green valley meadows called *heohematte* to pastures thousands of feet up in the alps. During the warmer weather, Swiss cheese was made. Petite, triangular-shaped cheese snacks wrapped in red and gold foil wrappers were available at the hotel. Guests and staff alike could sample the creamy brie.

Various times during the week, Meri and I would make the ten minute ride over to Oberried to see Melody. She also worked a split shift, spending most of her midday afternoons in the sun. Looking fabulous, I was jealous of her golden-brown tan. After complaints about work and aching feet, we'd get around to sharing the good time stories as well. I told her about a short hike we took to Blue Lake where the fish literally ate out of our hands. Melody was getting restless and ready to begin traveling again. It wasn't as easy for her to get away for quickie little side trips. By the end of the month, we planned to leave for Austria and then just travel exclusively the remaining four weeks in August.

On July twenty-forth, the gift shop attendant stopped by the dining hall. She wanted to tell Meri and me the U.S. spacecraft, with our three astronauts, landed safely back on earth. The news was good to hear and I was confident they would make it back. What a remarkable journey for them and they were alive to tell the world. Space travel would probably not happen in my lifetime but the Americans won the race to the moon, thanks to the dream of our former president.

Our Italian friends, we jokingly referred to as the guys from Illinois, came by in the afternoon. They were on their way to tour the local brewery. Rugenbrau, a large cave outside of town, had a continual supply of water from the mountain springs. The Rugen Brewery is well-known in many countries and most of the tourists look forward to their beer as part of the enjoyment of staying in Interlaken. Having no interest in tasting any beer, I went along for the walking tour with Raffaele and Carmelo. They dressed up for the outing, nylon shirts, and kerchiefs around their necks. We did enjoy being around these guys, even though they had a difficult time speaking English.

Melody came for a visit and after dinner a group from the Krone went out to the Belvedere Hotel, in Spiez. Co-workers,

Margaret and Bernadette Clemenz came along as well as three young teachers. Diane, Angus, and Bob, chaperons for the boys that week, were taking an evening break. Everyone spoke either English or German, and a steady discussion between the group ensued. No one seemed to mind making an extra effort in order to talk to one another. A couple of girls from Canada joined our table. As the conversation continued, they talked about going to England to look for work. Meri mentioned our leaving by week's end, and wondered if they would be interested in our positions. We certainly did not want to take off, without finding replacements. Crossing my fingers, I hoped these young women would consider staying on.

Frau Mooser hadn't been informed of our intentions of leaving. Inviting the Canadian girls over for an introduction, it was an opportune meeting and the timing could not have been better. She was agreeable with taking on these new staff members. Showing them around the hotel, we let them observe some of our work tasks and held a mini on-the-job training session. They met the kitchen staff and everyone seemed as excited as we were with the new maidens. The Hotel Krone owners and employes were wonderful and we had no intentions of leaving without notice and finding suitable workers. My prayers were answered, someone was watching out for us.

With only a few days left, once again we were bidding farewell to friends, guests, and staff at the hotel. The current group of school boys threw a going away party after the last supper of the evening. Ending with a big round of applause for amateur waitresses turned pro, we were then presented a wrapped box of Swiss candy. The teachers donated a bottle of wine, showing their appreciation for our steadfast endurance. Having a hard time holding back my tears, I looked toward Meri and she was already crying. The staff insisted on buying drinks at the Cabana Club and going dancing later at the Carlton. Our newest friends, who were strangers just a few weeks prior, joined the unexpected send off. Raffaele and Carmelo came by for the last dance and farewell. Unlike the final days in Frankfurt, the ending at Hotel Krone was a bit more emotional. The month went by so quickly and just as we were getting to know the co-workers and acquaintances, it was time to move along. Those ambivalent feelings surfaced once more as the good-byes became harder to handle.

August the first is a nationally celebrated holiday for all of Switzerland. Late in the thirteenth century, their political leaders formed an everlasting league of three central states with twenty-five cantons. Each province has its own distinct personality. Loyalties were especially deep and binding for the Independence Day. Banners adorned the whole town with a multitude of festivities happening in the streets. Meri and I helped decorate the lobby and the dining room. A parade with traditional folk dancers, bearded mountaineers and men in medieval military costumes lined the crowded roads. Nostalgic lyrics were sung by the natives and yodeling could be heard all over the valley.

I would miss the Swiss art scenes painted on the sides of buildings and the ornate hand carved window boxes filled with flowers. After dinner, we watched the fireworks show, much like our own country's fourth of July celebration. The pageantry and the folklore were elaborate and we felt privileged to be a part of the display and merriment.

The last evening could not have been more fitting as we said fond farewells to everyone. More hugs and a few more tears were exchanged. Working in Interlaken was fabulous even with the complicated work scheduling and sore tender feet. The monetary pay was more than fair and we received immeasurable benefits. Even grouchy Herr Mooser extended his hand in appreciation.

Meri and I packed on the morning we left and Melody got a ride over with a chalet employee. Each of us carried a small tote bag with a change of clothes, toiletries, and a beach towel. Those were the only possessions we would take for the month. A collection of gifts—from beer stein glasses to one-of-a-kind presents, insignificant trinkets to charms—were carefully wrapped in paper and boxed to be sent home. Everything else, from clothes to linens and other things, would go by train to the Luxembourg station and stored in a rented locker while we traveled. Mid-summer was fairly hot so we dressed in short culottes, light cotton shirts, and leather sandals. With the unexpected rains, we toted our knee-length trench-like raincoats in three different colors. Kelly green, royal blue, and beige were the popular shades of the day. I laughed at how little we were taking but we certainly didn't want to be loaded down with too much stuff.

By the time the precious cargo was sent, the magic noon hour came and went before we could get out of town. Why did it always take us so long to get organized? We were finally ready to jump into the great unknown, together we could face the best and the worst of any traveling. Having no idea what was ahead, it didn't much matter anymore.

After hitch-hiking for two months, we had it down to an art form. Melody even worked up a skit we performed to attract the attention of the passing traffic. Standing behind one another with thumbs and knees pointed toward the street, in unison we would toss our heads back, fling out our wrists, and flag down a driver. Most of the time, someone would stop within a matter of minutes. Sometimes there were other hitchhikers ahead and we'd have to patiently wait our turn in line. Usually it took longer for the guys to get rides but one time a car skipped a single male ahead of us and pulled over for three unwearied females. Sorry guys! However, due to the sheer number of our trio, some cars already had way too many passengers. I hated the less traveled side roads with few passing vehicles. During longer wait times, Meri would do the research for our next destination as I watched out for oncoming cars. Melody would entertain with her sarcasm. We were an awesome team!

St. Mark's Square, Venice

CHAPTER 7

—

SUNDAY, AUGUST 3

A young couple from Holland offered a lift out of Interlaken. They spoke English and had numerous questions about our intended travel plans. When it came time for the end of our ride, the Shalders insisted on buying drinks, and taking photographs. You would have thought we were celebrities, they were so intrigued with our tenacity. The next ride, on the way to Zürich, was with a man in a red Mustang. He was on holiday and told us he owned an engineering firm.

Nick Hayek was overtly friendly. He offered jobs if we ever decided to come back. Making a quick stop by some friends of his, this handsome couple invited everyone out to eat. Mr. Hayek purchased extra food to subsidize our coffers. He was such a nice guy! After dinner, he drove us to the home of one of Melody's co-workers from Oberried. We stayed in her families' residence, the first night out on the road. Later that evening, we headed out to a local disco club. The day was encouraging as everyone went out of their way giving support, donations, and assistance.

Breakfast was on the house and Melody's friend even took me to a small country chapel. After Mass, we only spent a short time visiting this mega city surrounded by wooded hillsides. Zürich is one of the principal centers in the world for international banking, group insurance companies and financing. The wealth was undeniable. Many elegant resorts, and fashionable spas, saturated this extremely classy area. Browsing through a few extravagant shops, and galleries, I didn't dare touch the merchandise. The prices were outrageous and I only had a few Swiss francs.

The last church we visited in Switzerland was St. Peter's Kirche. Displaying the largest clock tower in Europe, it was a fitting reminder this country is the world's largest watch producer. Bidding farewell to our Swiss friends, with the Matterhorn Mountain in the background, we said hello to another mountainous region. The majestic Republic of Austria was within our midst.

Two Austrian guys stopped at the borders edge. Members of a hard-rock band, one of the long haired hippies spoke English but the other did not. As I talked to Walter, he would intermittently try to translate our conversation to his friend. The musicians drove through one of the smallest countries in the world. Situated between Switzerland and Austria, Liechtenstein was one of those places that, if you blinked, you would miss the minuscule monarchy. The tiny Austrian House of Liechtenstein was a monetarily wealthy principality, despite its mini-dimensions. A lavishly rich prince, from the ruling family, lived in a bona fide castle. Schloss Vaduz, overlooked the capital city from high a top a mountain.

Almost seventy-five percent of the land in Austria is mountainous. High peaks and valleys, similar to the Swiss Alps, made up the most beautiful country I'd seen thus far. Our ride with the harmonious duo ended and another Austrian man stopped and took us on into Innsbruck. We only spent an hour in this popular Tyrolean sports town where the Olympic Games were held in 1964. Strategically located between high mountains, makes the area ideal for winter skiing. It didn't take long before three American service men stopped. Stationed in Stuttgart,

Germany, they were on leave and headed to Salzburg for the annual music and drama festival.

Just as we drove into Salzburg, the rain started to drizzle. The guys found the old seventh-century monastery where the Rodgers and Hammerstein movie *The Sound of Music* was filmed. The hills were truly alive with the songs of the Trapp family singers. No wonder the movie received best picture for the Academy Awards in 1965! Even in the light rain, you could see the gorgeous setting. The natural scenic backdrop of the Austrian Alps made an ideal location. Julie Andrews was perfect in her role as a singer and as a performer. As we walked around the wet grounds, I could almost hear her singing the world's best loved songs. Suddenly, without warning, a gush of rain poured down as we raced back to the car as fast as our legs would run. We were absolutely drenched!

For the next half-hour we drove around looking for a cheap place to spend the night. The only vacancy left was at an exclusive hotel. Meri was apprehensive about the high costs so one of the guys, Victor Engi, offered to pay for our lodging. They rented a two-bedroom suite for everyone. Sharing apples, crackers and peanuts with them, no one wanted to go back out into the storm. The guys provided some red wine as we sat around on the carpet, eating, and drinking, while sharing amusing stories about living in Europe. Although we were summer residents by choice, these guys were there due to an assignment for a military obligation. They were trying to make the best of their two years away from home. I was trying to make the best of a rainy night. The hotel was not too shabby and the guys were not bad looking either.

Having no trouble over-sleeping the next morning, we stayed up late. Peeking through the dark colored drapes, I could only see more clouds and rainfall. Having no idea what we would do in this city where Amadeus Mozart was born, our military roomies had to head back to the base. After checking out of the hotel, and dodging continual precipitation, we bought juice and croissants at the local market. Walking on to the train station, we needed a dry place to wait out the showers. Meeting a couple of cute guys from the States, they were going on tour of one of the neighboring salt mines. With no definite plans, we were invited to tag along. I proceeded to find a locker to store everyone's bags while Phil and Al rented a car. Taking off for the township of Hallein, it was only a short distance from Salzburg.

Austria is not a very large country, about the size of Maine, and once a part of the Holy Roman Empire. In fact, during the Hapsburg Dynasty, Austria ruled most of Europe for over six-hundred years. Austria and Hungary set up a powerful monarchy which ended at the conclusion of World War I. The Romans, the Franks, the Crusaders and other historic armies passed along the same roads we were traveling. Gazing out the car window, I viewed the same mountain range and terrain that ancient militia viewed before me. It was easy to let my imagination envision the armored soldiers, riding on horses through the valleys. The magnificent mountain surroundings reminded me of the great Colorado Rockies.

One of the wonderful things about travel, you are never quite sure of what you might see. I had absolutely no idea I would be going to so many grand, historic places in the old world. The planet Earth was covered with such an abundance of natural beauty. But there was something about the majesty of the mountains that captured my spirit. Not even the powerful oceans could stir my soul the way the mountains commanded attention. I could feel the presence of God!

Phil pulled the car to a halt into the parking lot outside the mines. After buying tickets, before entering the cave, we were fitted with white overalls worn over our clothes. Riding on the miners train, we traveled deep down into the cavern. The underground was cool and I was glad to have the added insulation. There didn't seem to be any danger involved, in this journey to the center of the earth, but I was still apprehensive. My tension mounted as the train kept going down farther and deeper. Looking back at Melody, I couldn't help but laugh as she rolled her eyes and poked fun at our new trendy outfits.

It was hard to take my eyes off the dreamy Austrian guide who led our group into the mine. Captivated by his flawlessly chiseled face, concentrating on his informative speech was difficult. Trying not to stare too long, he explained how salt deposits are excavated from beneath ground surfaces. Going into the many different chambers, he pointed out various tools and equipment used by the miners. There was an underground lake and some of the group got out of the train to float on the flat wooden rafts. Opting to stay in my seat, there was no way I was taking a chance falling into the water. Already feeling the soggy cold, I sat patiently and waited for the floaters as my thoughts drifted. I wondered how anyone could do this type of work every day. Sliding down through the salt shafts was fun but it might get monotonous on a daily basis. Riding the train back up the tracks was not as scary as going down. The light-colored suits didn't stay white for long; we were filthy dirty for the group pictures taken at the completion of the tour.

Phil and Al dropped us back by the train station before heading out of town. We gave up our expensive lodging since we weren't sure if we would be staying over another night. The popular musical commemoration continued with no vacancies anywhere. As the rain stopped, we ended up walking around the streets for hours, listening to the sounds of Mozart, Schubert, and Brahms. Having taken piano lessons as a young child, I recognized many of the melodies. The peaceful serene evening was the calm, after the storm, as we watched the bright lights and the people wandering about arm in arm. Both women and men and women and women clasped arms. Enjoying the summer festival while strolling in this notable city of music talents was definitely a serendipity.

Circling back to the train station, after several hours of hearing compositions, we retrieved our bags and sat down on a park bench. While munching on leftover bread and cheese, Meri chuckled at the possibility of sleeping out on the common grounds all night. A local woman, overhearing our potential dilemma, walked over and offered to rent a room in her home if we needed a bed.

With her mouth full of food, Melody was the first to say "yes" to the offer. Looking at one another in disbelief, we followed this angel to a bungalow not far away. The price was right and the bedroom made to order. There were two single beds and an antique divan just long enough for a short girl like me to stretch out. Sitting down to a round table covered with white doilies and china plates, our polite hostess served strudel pastry from her dining-room. Savoring the delicious Austrian treat, most of our dinners consisted of cheese, bread and fruit. Trying not to spend much money on food, it didn't hurt any of us to miss a few meals. We were working hard toward losing the extra pounds we'd gained the first two months of summer. How aggravating!

Waking up to the smell of strong coffee, we were offered sweet breads and jam for breakfast. I tried not to eat too much before hitting the streets but it tasted so good. With another day in Salzburg, we wanted to see some of the famous old churches, St. Michael's and the Franciscan Chapel. Someone once said, "If you've seen one church in Europe you've seen them all". But I never grew tired of walking through these elegant buildings. Catholic indoctrination pierced my very core!

Finding Mozart's Plaza, there was a monument built for him, by Ludwig Schwanthaler. Not far away were the Mirabell Gardens with skillfully overstated baroque landscaping. Life-sized marble statuettes, by the renowned Austrian sculptor Georg Raphael Donner, lined the grand staircase. With plenty of free art museums for viewing more paintings, statues and artifacts, the locals were happy to talk about their country and help out with directions. A good-humored tourist recommended we see the brilliant palace and gardens of Hellbrunn. This sizable estate, with designs from Italy, was fashioned by the first family who had Italian connections. The water park with decorated fountains and ponds were exceptional and worth the discretionary stop-over.

As the day got away, it was time to leave this lovely place and find our way to the authentic Italia. Disappointed that we couldn't go to Vienna, I wanted to see where the notorious Sigmund Freud lived and worked, developing his well-known psycho-analysis technique. The distance was too far from Salzburg, and with limited time and money, we had to be fairly selective. Meri kept the itinerary sensibly routed. Singing "Auf Wiedersehen" and "Good-bye" to Austria, we walked on to Italy.

Rides were easy and later in the afternoon a couple of young guys from Yugoslavia stopped. They were prepared to spend the night together whenever we were prepared to get a hotel. Melody made up a story, telling them we were married and waiting for our husbands to come back from Vietnam. I'm not sure they understood but Meri and I played along and eventually they gave up the quest. By the time we traversed the border into Italy, we were thoroughly bushed and sweaty.

Communication was next to impossible in this small Italian town, the name of which I could not pronounce. Before we found a suitable hotel, the midnight turned over. Other than the men hanging outside the lobby smoking cigarettes, the older building was clean and affordable. We were rented separate sleeping rooms with single beds and a shared bathroom at the end of the hall. While using the restroom, I looked around for toilet paper and couldn't even find a holder for any tissue. On the floor next to the stool were some old newspapers. After splashing cool water on my face, I fell fast asleep, despite the extreme heat and no window fan or coolers.

Waking up early to the sounds of people talking in the streets below, I awakened the girls to go shopping. Italians are known for their leather goods and we bought matching sandals to wear the remainder of the summer. Italian money conversion was a tad more complicated. One dollar equaled six-hundred and twenty lire. Melody criticized the abundance of paper currency and the assortment of numerous coins we had to carry. The mixes and sizes did bewilder counting and trading. Trying to keep track of correct amounts was problematic. Meri was convinced we were cheated out of exact change. It seemed to me like we were dealing with play money.

We stopped for morning caffelatte and biscotti. The late breakfast was needed to revive confused minds. Most Romans hurriedly drink their espresso while standing up at the bar. Sipping from my warm cup of flavored milk, I looked around the room and noticed it was true what others say about Italians.

Hands and arms were waiving in heated and loud conversations. While talking to each other, they seemed to be rather irritated about something. Such dramatic dialog!

Walking off in brand new Italian shoes, I found the path to Venice. By early afternoon, we arrived in the City on the Sea. It looked just like I expected from the many picture books and movie scenes. The main streets are lagoons and the numerous canals are connected by four hundred bridges. Transportation is either by foot or on boats and gondolas. The serenity is not disturbed by cars, trucks, or scooters. No motor vehicles are permitted in this distinctive location. Walking around St. Mark's Square, we could only glance through the doors of the Basilica, due to our exposed arms and legs. In this predominately Catholic country, women were permitted in the churches only if they dressed in skirts or slacks. No shorts or bare shoulders were allowed.

Old Venetian palaces were mystical, a unique blend of Renaissance Europe and the old Orient. Andrea Mantegna began Venetian art with the use of canvas as a material for painting. Canvases were mounted on stretchers and hung on walls in place of frescoes. This way the priceless art was protected from wet conditions, potentially damaging, especially in this city built over water.

In the back alleys we watched the legendary Murano glass blowers at work. After awhile, the smell of fresh garlic and onions stirred our appetites. Melody wanted to splurge on dinner. Sitting down at a sidewalk cafe, we ordered everything the waiter suggested. Bruschetta, fresh calamari, grilled eggplant, with bread and wine for three hungry gals. Salute to Venezia!

Relaxing with full stomachs, we watched the people feed the countless pigeons in the big square. I'd never seen so many pigeons in one place in my entire life. There were just as many flirtatious men strutting about and three cute guys managed to attract our attention. Melody gestured to one of them as they all walked over. A darling blond instantly caught my eye. Commenting on his light hair, Algero reminded me there were lots of Germans around Italy during and after the war. Smiling at his response, we continued talking about families. Eventually they asked if we would like to go for a boat ride on their shared motor craft docked a short distance from the piazza.

Floating on the Adriatic Sea, the warm, clear evening provided a perfect night for viewing the millions and millions of stars. Drifting into the shoreline at Lido Beach, we disembarked to take a walk on the sand. Embraced like lovers, everyone chatted and laughed while watching the sun go down. I listened to my two girlfriends giggling in the dark, as they played like children on the seashore. How could we possibly be spending a romantic nightfall on a coastline in Venice Italy? And was I really with a blue-eyed blond Italian? This certainly was a dream come true!

The following morning the guys made a surprise visit to our hotel. They walked with us to the ferry we had to ride back to the mainland. Watching Venice from afar, we started shouting in unison *"arrivederci"* to Roberto, Gianni, and Algero, as the vessel glided away. Etched in my memory forever would be the flawless marble statues, ornate gold palaces, and the conventional gondola singers. Napoleon described Venice as the "finest drawing room in all of Europe." As the music faded away, my thoughts drifted back to the glamorous night before, on the moonlit sand, with Algero. *Ti amo*!

Coming back to reality, after getting off the ferry, we took a ride with an older Italian man who was on his way to Florence, the capital of Tuscany. In this Art Center of the World, there are more famous painters, sculptors, architects, and composers, than from anywhere else. Italian artist Donatello, considered the greatest sculptor of the early Renaissance, introduced religious events through his statues. The busy city was bustling with hundreds of people, shoppers, and tourists alike. As we stepped out of the Mercedes, the driver handed us a card with his address and said to contact him when we got to Rome. He would love to be of service to help with any directions. The muggy afternoon left an odor of perspiration in the thick heavy air.

Tired and thirsty, we stopped off at a local bar for an orange soda before starting the search for a hotel. A tall, disheveled man in his early thirties was sitting at the next table. Interrupting our conversation, in his broken English, he offered to help with our lodging needs. He knew of a vacant cabin that he and his friends used during autumn harvest time. The cottage sounded like an appropriate place and we probably agreed too easily, but we were worn down from the extreme heat. Hermano drove us through Greve, a picturesque little village, some distance from Florence. Driving several more kilometers, he went pasts a row of cypress trees to a planted field high in the Tuscan Hills. Tiny towns and the patchwork landscapes of the numerous vineyards and olive groves covered the entire valley below. I thought I could smell the purple grapes!

Perched at the top of the hill, up a long, bumpy gravel road, was a small adobe hut. The shed had no framed glass windows but several round openings in the terracotta-colored clay structure. Rolling hills were covered with rows and rows of grapevines. Hermano repeated, as best he could, that the region had several wineries and most of the people in Greve worked at those facilities. Leaving us alone a while to unwind and clean up, Hermano drove back to town to buy some groceries.

Winery, Greve, Italy

There was no running water in the little building, so we bathed at a well not far from the hut. This place was as primitive as I cared to settle for an overnight stay. Hermano came back with food and two of his friends. Antonio and Michele spread white linen on the table as Hermano set out thick white bread, provolone cheese, grapes, watermelon, and Chianti wine. The most famous of the red wines are Chianti and it typically comes in a squat bottle wrapped in a straw holder. Grabbing the empty green bottle, I wanted it for a souvenir to use as a candle holder.

Communicating with these guys was a challenge, as we pointed and used pantomime talking. Melody made fun of them, as she often did, with men who couldn't understand her language. Most of the time, her sarcastic sense of humor and witty remarks were amusing. We all did know how to say *grazie* in Italian, thanking them for the food and drink. My appetite was ravenous!

Electricity in the house provided light and a small radio played music for our dining pleasure. After eating and drinking a few glasses of wine, Antonio asked me to dance. I insisted everyone dance in the small crowded space. Bumping into each other and laughing out of control, I'm not really sure what was so funny. The guys could tell we'd had too much to drink and they left us alone. Hermano promised to come back in the morning and give us a ride. Thank you, Jesus!

Beds were molded into the walls and consisted of a thin pad on a rock-hard surface. The stucco compartment reminded me of the home of the Flintstones. No covers were needed in the balmy weather. Laying my towel over the stone cot, I tried to get some sleep. When given a free place to stay, I hated to complain, but the heat was truly unbearable. Adapted to hot and humid summers, I certainly could have used a draft to dry off the dripping beads of sweat. My whole body glowed!

Most days we were in a continual state of apprehension. Wondering, out loud, we could only hope for pleasant rides and clean lodging. Usually everything turned out in our favor but there were always some fears associated with not knowing what was in store. Each night as we talked about the day's events, we couldn't help but speculate what tomorrow would bring. We saw

Europe in ways I didn't think possible. For the most part, the people were more than hospitable.

Hermano returned in the morning, driving us back to Greve. He had friends who would take us into Firenze. Maria, a plump middle-aged lady, and her lovely teenage daughter offered to help. Christina spoke English and she mentioned several places we would want to visit while in the city of Florence. On the way to town, she suggested starting our day in the central-market district. Every Italian city had its own distinct atmosphere. The birthplace of the Renaissance, was nothing like Venice. From the midpoint drop-off, we walked the square to the Basilica of St. Lawrence (San Lorenzo) built by sculptor-architect Filippo Brunelleschi early in the fifteenth century.

Once one of the richest cities in Europe, the Florentine cloth finishing industry flourished during the 1400s. During that epoch, the city was over-populated with a large number of the most talented artists in all of Europe. Under the stern rule of the powerful Medici family, Florence prospered throughout the century. The Medici Chapel was housed inside the Basilica. Deceased members, of the most important political family of Florence, were also buried inside the church. This mausoleum to the Medici family was astounding. Not surprising, we learned it was designed and built by Michelangelo with the help of his students.

Passing by the Piazza della Signoria, we continued on our tour to the famous Academia Gallery, where Michelangelo's greatest effort of genius stands. The bigger than life statue of David, said to be "the perfect man," was absolutely impeccable. The nude figure seemed to be the most common expression that suited Michelangelo Buonarroti. With way too many churches, art galleries, and museums for our happy feet to walk in and out, we had to take a much needed break.

No matter how drained we felt, going shopping could revitalize our energy. Buying gifts at the outdoor flea markets became addictive. We needed our daily fix! Procuring leather gloves for me, and a leather covered bottle for my dad, those were my only purchases. There were scores of things I wanted to buy but I had to control my spending. In fact, the only way I was able to buy anything was because of all the free accommodations bestowed our way.

Before leaving the states, Meri bought the book *Europe on 5 Dollars a Day* (it was in her travel case that was stolen). Turns out we didn't need the paperback guide book after all. Meri bragged she could rewrite the volume and tell her readers how to travel in Europe for only pennies a day. We considered ourselves lucky to be getting by so economically.

When Hermano finished working, he met us at the Duomo, the largest cathedral in the world. Santa Maria del Fiore is considered the crown jewel of Florence. Next to the cathedral was the Campanile Tower covered with pink, green and white marble tiles. Before driving back to Greve, he stopped to pick up a pizza. Devouring this authentic Italian meal, originally introduced in Naples, Italy, completed our visit of the most popular city in the Tuscan region. *Buon giorno*!

After eating, we headed back down the hill to a Friday night dance in Greve. As strangers in this small village town, we certainly attracted plenty of attention. Being the only blue eyed, blonds, surrounded by brown-eyed brunettes, everyone glanced our way. The open air dance in the plaza was a blast but the guys were getting a bit too chummy. Several hours of dancing were exhausting and I was ready to retire back to the hut. Hermano insisted we come to another dance on Saturday night. Agreeing to his request, we had no intentions of staying over the weekend.

Greve was an enjoyable place but we needed to move on to Rome. Besides, I was feeling very grubby and needed a real bath. There were field mice running around the hillside making us rather squeamish. The next day, in the early morning hours, we left unannounced. In the scorching heat, we walked a mile down the dusty gravel road to the paved but secluded street. However, our inconsiderate appreciation for Hermano's kindness came back to haunt us.

Hitchhiking turned disastrous in this remote farmland, where cars were few and far between. Most of the rides were with "dirty old men" and I do mean icky. Small cars forced one of us to sit in the front seat close to the driver. Trying not to look, I had to sit next to a creep who took the liberty of "playing with himself." One older man fondled with Meri's leg and another slimy guy tried to put his hand up Melody's blouse. None of them could speak English but we knew they understand the word "no." After getting away from the pervert with the roving hands, to add perversion to insult, a newer sports car pulled up skidding to a halt. Thinking he might be a safe ride, we walked over to his car and the sneaky snake had his pants unzipped, exposing himself.

Melody finally broke down and started to cry. What was up with these Italian men? Another odd character stopped and we hesitantly climbed into the back seat. Meri detected guns and rifles under the cushions we were sitting on. He didn't talk to us and we didn't try to talk to him either. Relieved when we finally got out of that car, I was sure he was a member of the mafia. By this time, everyone was a little "gun shy" (no pun intended) about taking any more rides with males. At this point, I was regretting we didn't buy the summer train passes. We feared for our lives!

Once we arrived in Rome, while walking down a crowded street, a pack of boys gathered around like dogs in a heat. The whole day was scary and weird. Most of our hitchhiking experiences went well until landing in central Italy. Innocent flirting was tolerable, but the touching without our permission and the whistling and pestering were making me uneasy. Italy was a rough country! Spotting a YMCA sign nearby, we darted in and were able to get beds for the night in the girl's dormitory. Safe at last, I took a long hot shower to try and gain back some of my composure.

Feeling secure in this sanitary building, the bathroom had toilet tissue and the beds had sheets. Emotionally drained, none of us wanted to go back out to eat for fear of being attacked by a herd of wild beasts. Sitting on the bed, lethargically eating bread, cheese and water, we waited for our wet hair to dry. It didn't take long to calm down and start to see some humor in the twisted day. Laughing became contagious as I started to giggle in disbelief at the bizarre rides and everything we had to endure. Laughter was definitely good medicine and a great way to alleviate tension. At least we were out of harms way and could eat in peace and solitude. Our three guardian angels were certainly working overtime. Tomorrow would have to be a better day!

Meri picked up the travel guide and mentioned places of interest for touring. As Melody and I listened, we were usually in agreement as to what we wanted to see. Rome, the capital of Italy, was the largest and most populated metropolis. This city of the seven hills had more to see than most of the other places we'd been. Planning on staying several days, the next day was Sunday. Suggesting we go first to the Vatican, I reminded everyone to wear their dresses. Most of the day would be spent in churches and we had to dress appropriately. I borrowed a dress from Melody.

Washing out clothes by hand every evening was part of our nightly routine. The warm summer temperatures provided enough heat to hang dry our laundry. We'd drape panties over the backs of chairs or bathroom towel racks. Clean lingerie was ready to wear by morning. Gazing out the back window of the dorm room, I noticed strings of clothes hung in the outside air. Chuckling, I told the girls we'd been doing laundry "Italian style." Shirts, pants, skirts, and underwear were hooked to ropes by clothespins, hanging up and down the sides of the buildings. The whole back alley way was covered in a menagerie of garments. Now that's Italian!

St. Peter's Square, Vatican

CHAPTER 8

—

SUNDAY, AUGUST 10

While paying for our sleeping beds, before stepping out into the jungle, the front desk clerk offered an impending tip. He said it was not prudent for women to travel alone while in Rome. *No kidding*, I thought. If we could find a trusted man for accompaniment, other men would respect our privacy. After breakfast, we cautiously started walking toward the Vatican.

It was a day of rest for the more aggressive men, as we were watched by three Italian militia. Meri motioned to them with a camera in hand; she wanted a group photo, in front of the most celebrated Basilica. The enormous oval piazza of St. Peter, designed by Lorenzo Bernini, was the perfect setting. Once the picture was taken; we were invited to attend Mass in the cathedral. Since these guys were dressed in uniforms, Melody insisted we needed their protection as military escorts.

The Basilica was the most astounding church I had ever seen. Michelangelo's greatest artistic achievement, the *Pieta*, was poised at the entry vestibule. The life-like carving of the Blessed Mary, holding her beloved Son, was profoundly touching. Everything, from the marble floors to the hand painted ceilings, was exquisite. The building was decorated with tons of treasures and an enormous variety of arts. The statues and sculptures seemed to be in perfect harmony with one another. Infinite amounts of priceless paintings adorned every corner of the majestic cathedral. Nothing short of remarkable, we were deeply impressed by such a glorious and holy place. The pictures, and the many messages sent from the eminent saints, reminded me of God's glory.

Various Masses were going on at the same time in different areas of the massive building. We spent several hours touring these chambers that were beyond description. Going down a hidden staircase, we entered the burial rooms of numerous past Popes. Simon Peter, one of the apostles of Jesus and the first Bishop of Rome, is presumed buried in this notable place for his namesake. Feeling overwhelmed, we needed a respite from looking at the crypts and vaults of the dead.

For lunch, the guys recommended a restaurant called Old Rome. After ordering a Panini sandwich with thick mozzarella cheese and thinly sliced prosciutto ham, there was always room for gelato. The creamy ice milk was a treat I could not deny myself. Diet or not!

Leaving Vatican City, we passed by Castle Sant' Angelo, once used as a fortress for the Popes. Walking over another architectural masterpiece, the bridge crossing the Tiber River led to the Colosseum. In old ancient grandeur, the colossal Flavian Amphitheater is one of the most well-known ruins in the entire world. Surviving almost two-thousand years, shaped like a giant football stadium, it could once seat over forty-five thousand spectators. However, the Romans did not prefer nonviolent sports. They watched fights between gladiators and attacks on men by wild animals. Rome did combine the ancient, the medieval, and the modern, into one city.

Next to the Colosseum is the Arch of Constantine, awarded to this emperor after a military victory. During the reign of Constantine I, in the fourth century, Christianity became the official religion of the Holy Roman Empire. Across from the Colosseum were the Temple of Venus and the Temple of Rome.

These were considered the leading and most splendid of Rome's temples. The Arch of Titus, erected after that emperor's death, was to commemorate the capture of Jerusalem. The famed Roman Forum contains a series of monuments constructed over a period of one-hundred and fifty years. Surrounding the area were Forums to Julius Caesar, Augustus, and other celebrated leaders. Volumes have been written describing the aged remains, above the ground, in the ground and under the ground, all over this ancient city. Tremendous amounts of past could be seen, in every direction, as far as the eye could see. All roads came back to Rome!

By nightfall, we were worn out from walking and looking at so many old rocks and buildings. A movie sounded like fun and the guys treated us to an Italian film. Although their dates could not understand the words, after a long day of sightseeing, the chance to rest our weary minds and bodies were what we needed. After the show, Domenico Forte and his friends walked us back to the YMCA. These educated officers were polite and true gentlemen, nothing like the low life men from the previous day. I thanked the desk clerk for his excellent advice and told him of our escorts. Without any incidents, we made it through the streets of Rome. It was a good day!

Wanting to find a place to stay in a nicer part of town, we checked out of the Y before starting day two of the Roman holiday tour. Walking by The Vittoriano, the grandiose monument is to Victor Emmanuel II, celebrating Italian independence. A promenade in the piazzas was a favorite pastime for many people, as they marveled at the priceless palazzos (buildings) and fountains that dazzled the courtyards. Morning market was open for business at the Piazza of Campo De' Fiori. The vibrant bazaar showed off a variety of foods, gifts and works of art. After "just looking," we took a stroll through Villa Borghese, a natural landscaped park, in the heart of downtown Rome.

With renewed stamina, we did what girls do best, window shopping in a rather expensive area. Recognizing the name of the street, it was the same via as the address we were given by a driver. I mentioned we should try to find his place of business.

While peering through a shop window, the owner of the fabric store came out the door to greet us. The well-dressed man, aware of whom we were, introduced himself as Wladimiro Pucciarini. He attempted to tell me he and his cousin had a cottage and we were welcomed to stay a while. Looking at Meri and Melody, they didn't give me any signs of opposition. Humbly accepting his liberal proposal, he led the way to his car. Riding again in his black Mercedes, he drove to the coast outside of Rome. The dwelling was nothing extravagant, just a modest seaside bathhouse on the Riviera. I couldn't stop smiling!

Mr. Pucciarini suggested going to dinner by the sea. Stopping at an outdoor restaurant on the waterfront, he ordered our meals since we couldn't interpret the menu. The first course was an antipasti dish that included olives, grilled vegetables, artichoke hearts and pecorino cheese. Then the waiter served bistecca, (steak) with spaghetti pasta on the side (no tomato sauce) and vino (red table wine). The grand finale was a delicious tiramisu. After taking my last bite, I sat back in my chair and thought how privileged I was to be in Rome, doing what the Romans do.

This refined man seemed enthralled in our travel plans. Knowing few English words, he kept apologizing for his ignorance. Toting a small Italian-English dictionary, he continually looked up words he wanted to translate in his speaking. This meal was definitely very long and drawn out. We were in no hurry; I was thoroughly enjoying the ambiance and the conversation.

After dinner, Wladi, as he preferred to be called, took a drive back in to Rome so we could get a glimpse of some other sites. Viewing Rome at night, with lights on the old and new, provided a new perspective of the city. The Sound and Light Spectacle in the Roman Forum was impressive. Having our own personal tour guide and chauffeur, we saw the most important places. Driving on to Circus Maximus where at one time over 200,000 spectators watched Roman chariot races. Today, there are scores of shops and restaurants, as the locals and tourists spend time taking in the night life. Sitting down at an outdoor table, we consumed a glass of wine before driving to the beach house. Meri and Melody would not stop grinning at me, seated in the front with Wladi.

Sleeping in late the next day, Melody was the first to get up. She opened the curtains as bright sunlight flooded the room. It was time to get out on the beach. Wearing shorts and a tee shirt, I didn't replace my stolen swimsuit. Wladi wanted to buy me a new two piece after I told him the story of my loss. Having a bathing suit was not a priority; I was only interested in keeping my legs and arms tanned. Mr. Pucciarini was already doing enough and he didn't need to buy me anything. With a glass of frizzante (sparkling water) in hand, I proceeded to get drunk on sunshine.

Assuming this man to be in his early forties, he said he'd never been married. His hectic business demands took him away from home on a regular basis. Expressing his contentment in spending time with three attractive American women, he took delight in our companionship. Speaking as much with his hands, as with words, he reassured us we were no burden. He was splurging and indulging because it pleased him. After soaking up a few hours of vitamin D, we showered and got ready for more sightseeing. We were off on another first class tour of Italy's finest ruins.

Wladi drove quite aways to the Catacombs of St. Calixtus. The atypical tour, covered many miles of rocky mazes. Long passageways meandered underground and branched out into small rooms. Martyred popes and Christians, from the third century, were buried on the different levels in the secretive grotto. The earliest Christian drawings could be seen on the ancient walls. There were frescoes portraying the Sacraments and other religious inscriptions. These first Christians had to pave the way for the rest, using the Catacombs for places of secret worship, when hiding from Roman soldiers. A life without religious freedoms was hard to consider. Even in Europe, where Christianity had been in a crisis, we walked in and out of the churches without fear of any inquisition. I couldn't help but feel tremendous compassion for these early Christian martyrs.

Driving down the old Roman Road, we came to the elegant basilica of San Paulo, (St. Paul) the second largest church in

Rome. Supposedly this structure is built over the tomb of the Saint. The intact, interior walls were covered with colorful mosaic portraits, of several more past popes. Then Wladi drove south of Rome, in the Alban Hills, to the outskirts of Castel Gandolfo, the summer resident of Pope Paul the VI, where he spent most holidays. Tourists were not allowed access anywhere close to this dwelling. A visit to the Pantheon was next on the agenda, ranking as one of the greatest masterworks of Roman Architecture. Originally built as a Roman temple, it was later consecrated as a Catholic Church. Meandering past the great bronze doors, this superb circular room was referred to as the "Temple of all the gods." Outside, in the Piazza della Rotunda, was a multitude of motor scooters parked along side the buildings.

Within walking distance was the Piazza Di Spagna or Spanish Steps. This popular tourist's attraction is the longest, and widest, staircase in Europe. At the base of the steps is La Fontana della Barcaccia, Fountain of the Old Boat, and at the top, the chapel Trinita dei Monti. Many young people and sightseers swarmed up and down the steps and in the surrounding district.

After a short tour, we dined in another fabulous restaurant. Finding out the Italians eat more than pasta and pizza, we had a choice from excellent soups, cheese and sausage hors d'oeuvres, tasty fish or chicken dishes with luscious pastries and creamy frozen desserts. After several hours of drinking, talking, and consuming food, we went to see the notoriously romantic, Trevi Fountain.

Arriving at Piazza di Trevi, just as the night sky emerged, a myriad of couples and lovers were milling about. Throwing three coins in the fountain, supposedly, this would ensure my return to the Eternal City. Before heading back to the beach apartment, Wladi drove to a high plateau. At the top of this winding road was a beautiful night-time view of Rome. The unexpected sight, and the extraordinary day, closed with an incredible vision of the Capital of the world. *Bellissima*!

The following morning, our model host announced he had to leave for Paris on business. After breakfast, we would have to go. It was a sad departure and Signore Pucciarini requested letters, and photos, once we returned to the states. His lavish generosity enabled visiting places in Rome we'd never gotten to see otherwise. Giving a personal thanks, to this special man from Italy, he told me he would never forget my dark blue eyes that reminded him of the Mediterranean Sea.

Rides going away from Italy were much more acceptable than the rides into the Roman city. Meri thought it would be interesting to see the Leaning Tower of Pisa. This port city lies at the junction of two rivers by the sea. The Piazza dei Miracoli, the "Square of Miracles" is where the famed slanted bell tower stands, alongside other grand churches. The main cathedral has a special place in Italian architecture due to the harmonious relationship between the other churches, the freestanding tower and the baptistery. Pisa is also the birthplace of the physicist and astronomer, Galileo. The salty atmosphere of the Mediterranean climate surrounded the maritime seaport.

While pacing about, gawking at the tower and other amazing structures in the plaza, a young student came over and introduced himself. He proceeded to tell us he studied at the university that specialized in research and the education of graduate students. Then he extended an invite to a party. When Meri told him we hadn't found a place to stay for the night, he quickly offered the use of the apartment he shared with a roommate. On the way to Federico's home, we took a walk down by the waterfront. He explained the Laguna once served as a base, for old Roman naval expeditions, but in more recent history, access to the sea had become increasingly difficult.

Melody was somewhat concerned, wondering if this guy could be trusted. We were taking lots of risks with accepting rides and lodging from strangers. I'm sure we were probably too trusting and so far nothing had happened we couldn't handle. Our pocketbooks had much more to do with our opting to be scavengers than making wise decisions. Setting aside a certain amount of money each day, if we lucked out with complimentary food or lodging, then we had more cash for shopping.

The so called "party" turned out to be the three of us and a couple of friends of Federico's. Our amiable host, along with

Roberto and Carlo, brought pizza to share while we listened to records, danced, and chatted the evening away. These charming scholars were well educated and well versed about historic information. Although they were not as good-looking as some of the other Italians we'd met, they could speak English and offered intellectual conversation and humor.

At least Federico was sophisticated enough to provide a separate room for sleeping. Appreciating resting alone, I could look pretty scary in the early mornings when first waking up. Avoiding most everyone, I had to wash my oily hair and put on some make-up before I was presentable.

Up and out early the next day, we were hoping to grab a little sun time along the way. Tan legs always looked better in shorts. However, on the beach in Viareggio, the Italian guys swarmed the area like honeybees. If it were not so hot, I would have worn jeans to ward off the annoying wasp. These guys were savages and I was certainly ready to leave Italy and the maddening men. Ciao baby!

Getting away from the beach was next to impossible. Most passing cars were packed with many passengers. Finally a young couple offered a ride along the Riviera. They stopped in Genoa, the birthplace of Christopher Columbus. Two respectable Italian men, working for IBM, drove us on to their home town of Sanremo, the city of flowers. One of the gentlemen offered his garage, as long as we didn't mind the hard surface for sleeping. Although it didn't sound too appealing, darkness circled the night sky and a torrential rain came pouring down. We were very grateful to get in out of the weather. He brought out some blankets for our use which helped to alleviate the uncomfortable floor.

Resting was not the greatest on the concrete interior. Waking up early, already dressed, we left our crude slumber room and sauntered out onto the busy street. Directly behind this city on the Med, were the mountains of the Maritime Alps. An older gentleman, sitting at a sidewalk café, bought cappuccino and almond pastries for three hungry girls. While we ate, he said August the fifteenth was a national holiday for Italy. Most shops would be closed as everyone headed to the beach for the day. Thanking him for the food and info, we moseyed toward the autostrada.

The traffic was terrible, bumper-to-bumper cars in both directions. Along the roadside were large numbers of hitchhikers. Just as we got in line for a ride, a paddy-wagon drove up and motioned the half-dozen or so backpackers to climb into the rear of the van. No tickets issued this time! Driving on down the motorway, we were dumped off in a less congested area. A car with two young Italians quickly stopped. These darling guys sang with the pop group Up with People. I was forced to change my unimpressed opinion about these Italian men. Some of them were totally obnoxious but others were positively angelic. The remainder of the day we were treated as special guests by the sweet singing Giovanni Mangione, and his colleague and accompaniment.

Driving on to Monte Carlo, the wealthiest and most romantic tourist resort in Monaco, we were driven around this posh area by our personal guides. Passing the palace where Grace Kelly lived, they drove on to the world renowned, casino. The gambling attracts the rich and famous from all over the world. Docked in the harbor were big cruisers and mega-yachts with impressive wooden sailboats floating in the waters off the Mediterranean. Expensive dress shops lined the water front but the only thing we could afford was the pleasure of watching the well-dressed people.

As the singing duo said farewell, near the entrance of the casino, they insisted on taking names and addresses. One day soon, they would come to America and find us. After they drove away, we talked to a man on the sidewalk, standing next to a classic Royals Royce car. He offered some helpful hints for tourists who wanted to tour the grand casino. As we turned to leave, Meri timidly asked him who he was driving around? Quietly disclosing his chauffeur status for Princess Grace, he went on to say she was outside the kingdom and he was waiting on another passenger.

Wandering into the casino, we turned and walked out, as fast as we entered. Shorts and sandals weren't really appropriate attire in the fancy gambling enterprise. We continued to work our way around the French Riviera, as this impressive drive along the coast flaunted large rocks and lots of pine, and palm trees by the waters edge. Looking at this paradise, from the car, it was hard to imagine France as the battle ground for most of World War I and much of World War II. The light of day was fading fast, as our ride came to an end on the outskirts of the city of Marseilles.

Desperate to get closer into town to locate a hotel, we foolishly took a ride with three males. Setting some ground rules early on, we agreed not to hitchhike after sunset and never with more than two men, in the car, at the same time. These guys with dark complexions, probably about our age, spoke no English. After throwing our luggage in the trunk, Meri crawled in the front seat between two of the young teenagers and Melody and I climbed in the back with the other scrawny kid.

These perky adolescent boys talked to each other, in French, acting rather brazen. Although we were dubious this time, we kept reassuring each other the guys were probably harmless and we didn't have far to go. Meri could comprehend some of what they were saying and she feared we might be headed for trouble. Abruptly stopping, the driver turned down a dirt road on the fringe of town. Ending up in an abandoned field, the driver turned off the car and everyone got out. We were not sure what they had in mind; Melody screamed that she was going for help. Yelling loudly, she raced back up the road. Trying to stay calm, hoping to reclaim our things, I started to pray. God help us!

One of the guys grabbed my arm, pushed me up against the dusty car and tried to kiss me. He was talking to me in French as I talked to him in English. Turning my head away from his face, I pointed to the trunk of the car, requesting my things and my ultimate release. The exchange was rather ludicrous, neither understanding what the other was saying. Meri was trembling, noticeably upset, while going through the same scenario with one of the other guys. She stammered, trying to verbalize the right words in French, asking him to hand over our belongings and please let her go. Not that we cared about the clothes, but our passports and money were also in the trunk.

Melody flagged down a passing automobile and within minutes, I could see the car headlights moving through the darken grasslands. As the vehicle approached, the guys hurriedly opened the trunk, flung out our things on the ground, and sped away. The bewildered family stopped, checking to make sure we were unharmed, then offered to drive us to the police station.

With the help of the Good Samaritans, we tried to tell the authorities what had transpired. The officer spoke little English and probably didn't comprehend the whole story. Obviously shaken, by the ordeal, Melody was positive we were close to being molested. If not for the immediate aid from the young couple, with two small children, the night could have been devastating. Sitting in the stillness, of the closed-door office, I thanked God that the joyride was over. We were spared!

With Italy on holiday, there were no vacancies at any of the local hotels. The sympathetic police officer called a convent and made arrangements for our stay there for the night. He dropped us off at the Assumption House of Sisters, where we were greeted at the door by a petite elderly nun. Speaking in French, she showed the way through the rectory, making sure we were familiar with her church home. Trying to console our spirits, after handing out pillows and bedding, she took my hand and pulled me toward the kitchen. Dishing up soup with French bread, we sat down to eat on wooden benches alongside the dining table. Blessing me with the sign of the cross, she waved goodnight as Meri thanked her in French. Melody and I repeated in unison, "*Merci, merci.*"

While getting ready for bed, I couldn't help but chuckle at the whole episode occurring earlier in the evening. I honestly don't think the guys meant any real harm; they were feeling frisky and hoped we would go along with their plans of fooling around. At least they didn't drive off with our passports and pittance of cash. So far we'd been blessed, for the most part, with good quality rides (except one day in Italy) and something like this was bound to happen sooner, if not later. On that particular night, I prayed even harder for our continued safety and survival.

Waking up early to the sounds of bells ringing, I attended Mass before breakfast. Especially grateful for the day, I took another opportunity to thank God for all my blessings. The same lovable nun handed out sweet croissants and café before hugging and blessing us one last time. Outside the convent walls, in the light of day, we were able to see a large commercial port city.

On an island in the bay was an old castle that had been converted into a prison. Feeling edgy, in this city of gangsters, we didn't want to spend any more time where a potentially disparaging encounter almost occurred. Lacking confidence and motivation, sticking out our hesitant thumbs, two young French guys pulled over. They were headed to Spain on holiday, and would gladly go to Barcelona. Or maybe they were going to Barcelona, because that was where we wanted to go.

Stopping along the way, we picnicked on the side of the road. Meri chatted with the guys who spoke some English. Most of the time, I did enjoy the conversations and getting to know these strangers we'd never see again. While munching on fruit and cheese, they mentioned Woodstock. Everyone had heard about the three-day rock music festival scheduled to happen in New York. Meri was disappointed she wasn't there for the big love-in. Reflecting on the moment, I was exactly where I wanted to be, drifting through Europe while creating my own groovy happening.

Later in the week, we learned four-hundred thousand young people attended the historic but peaceful event. They camped out at a large dairy farm, over a rainy three day weekend, in the Catskill Mountains resort town of Bethel. Thirty-two well-known musicians appeared, to a counterculture group of concert enthusiasts for "An Aquarian Exposition." What a great moment in history!

CHAPTER 9

—

SUNDAY, AUGUST 17

Andre and Claude reached Barcelona, Spain's second largest city, by late afternoon. This very multiethnic, urban area, is said to be the cultural capital of Spain. Appealing shops and colorful restaurants filled the busy community as we passed by a monument to Christopher Columbus.

Melody tried to find her cousins, who supposedly lived in the vicinity, hoping for a free place to stay. She was not able to locate them and because we were exceedingly low on cash, the guys offered the use of their car. They were more than happy to accommodate our lodging needs and after driving to a meager camping facility, their mini-auto became a bed for outdoor camping.

Sleeping in cars was not conducive to happy camping. In the drive-in campsite were outdoor shower stalls and changing facilities. After breakfast, we went to the American Consulate, to try and find the address for Melody's relatives. Learning they lived in a town much farther south, we didn't have time to go the extra distance. Melody could go to her cousins after Meri and I returned to college. She wasn't going back to school and was planning to stay on another month. Wiring home for money, she would pick up her much needed cash on the way back from England.

While waiting on Melody, the office attendant passed on the news of Hurricane Camille. The devastating storm hit Louisiana and Mississippi, killing several hundred people and leaving many thousands homeless. At least we weren't forced to sleep on the beach because of no home!

Leaving the office, we walked on to Pueblo Spain, an area designed in 1929 for their Universal Exposition. Meant to illustrate the various architectural styles of Spain, the highlight for everyone was the complex Church of Sagrada Familia. Built in the eighteen-hundreds, this ornate structure, with decorated mosaic towers on the outside, had a luminous nativity scene on display inside. The artistic work of designer Antoni Gaudi was superb and he dedicated one of the principal towers to the Blessed Virgin Mary. Equally as splendid was the exquisitely built Santa Eulalia Gothic Cathedral, the seat of the Archbishop of Barcelona.

We couldn't visit Spain without seeing one of the celebrated bullfights. As we entered the arena, you could hear the shouting and screaming fans. Bullfighting, the national sport of Spain, is regarded as a fine art. In the ring were three matadors, their assistants, and six, proud long-horns, prancing around the ring. One of the horseback riders lanced the bull with a spear to weaken him. The matador made a few slow passes, with his red cape, before ultimately stabbing the bull to death. Cheering crowds clapped as the bull fell to the ground. The blood and cruelty of the sport was rather sickening! I certainly was not in my element.

Evening meals in Spain are long and drawn out. The custom is to eat late and make the meal last a few hours. Most of the restaurants didn't even open until after nine o'clock. Starved by the time we ate, not accustomed to these extended dinners, I gulped down my food in a few minutes. The guys talked about camping out on the sand near the beach. Anything had to be better than another night of a cramped siesta in a compact car. Flexibility was my newly acquired talent!

It took awhile to find Costa Brava campground, the darkened skies didn't help. The sea breeze and the sounds of the waves were calming but that was the only fond memory of that beach. Andre set up a small tent for sleeping but the mosquitoes were so thick, between the buzzing and swatting, I was up all night. And if that were not enough interruptions, security patrol came by at three in the morning for passport checks. Needless to say, it was another sleepless night in Spain.

As we left the seashore, the car was making audible signs of mechanical troubles. Eventually breaking down in an unknown tourist's town, we couldn't patiently wait for car repairs. Trying to get a ride was impossible; no one was leaving the shoreline in the blistering weather. Driving away from the hot spot in a taxi, we abandoned Andre and Claude to deal with the overheated car. Back out on the highway, two guys from Canada stopped and gave us a lift to Beziers France. By the time the frustrating day ended, we'd hardly covered any distance before night fell.

Meri stopped a woman on the street, asking her where the closest hotel was located. The nice lady insisted we stay with her as she motioned to the direction of her home. After the unforeseen cost of the taxi fare, this was music to my ears. Never planning on any complimentary rooms, we appreciated any free bed. Over spending, on too many shopping sprees and gifts, we welcomed any concessions on lodging expenses. Mel was almost broke and Meri and I were low on funds.

After two nights with little to no sleep, I slept like a bear. Stretched out on a flat surface, in a dark room was my most preferred sleeping style. In the quiet bedroom, I woke up to the familiar smell of freshly brewed coffee. Scrambled eggs and homemade bread were waiting on the table, as we prepared to start another day. Once again, I had to rethink my negative thoughts about the rude and arrogant French people. This gregarious little lady was an absolute sweetheart and a perfect hostess.

On the road again, we had a really long day of travel through France, as we headed to the U.K. As one might expect, now that we were in a hurry to see as much as we could, in the short amount of time left, hitchhiking was not going well. Not only were rides sparse, a couple of prying policemen, on bicycles, stopped to confirm identifications. The day was exasperating! Too much time was wasted, standing around waiting in the sweltering August sun. Reaching Lyon just as darkness blanketed the town, we still had hundreds of kilometers to go before the border.

Sulking along the street, a young business man came out of his office, initiating a conversation. He was on his way to Paris and if we didn't mind driving in the dark, he would be happy to have company. This solitary man drove nonstop, until the wee hours of the morning, as I tried to sleep while sitting up. Before checking into a hotel, at four o'clock, Mr. Stud stopped to pick up a female companion. The floozy looking lady hopped in the front seat and never stopped talking. He obviously knew her as she questioned him about his three passengers. Barely able to respond, I tried to muster a smile when she turned around to look at me over her left shoulder.

Another wasted morning, sleeping until almost noon, the time we saved on the overnight ride didn't help our cause. I suppose we needed the beauty rest! Reaching Calais by late afternoon, we caught the ferry crossing the English Channel, on the way to the United Kingdom. Costing two and a half pounds, the seven dollar boat-ride was an unexpected expense. Now Melody was completely out of money and Meri and my resources were dwindling. I'm not sure what we would have done, if it were not for the charitable donations. After boarding, two of the ship's crew members offered drinks in their cabin quarter. Taking pity on our scanty situation, if we returned the following Tuesday, they wouldn't charge for the ride back over. We promised to see them in a week.

Low forming clouds prohibited any clear views of the bay but I noticed straight away, all the road signs were in English. I could actually read directions again. By the time we reached Dover, it was almost dark and a youth hostel was conveniently located close by. Usually the hostels were on the far-side of town, making them difficult to find. Meri and Melody stayed for free, as my first-time guests, at the pension.

There were several Canadian and American girls staying in the boarding house rooms. Talking to them, without struggling, I could understand every word. In the common lounging quarters, everyone was discussing the tragic murder of actress Sharon Tate. Shocked to hear the gruesome details of this senseless massacre, I wondered why anyone in their right mind would want to kill these people in her California home. Recalling the movie *Valley of the Dolls*, I remembered how beautiful she was. Someone said she was eight months pregnant at the time of her death.

The seagulls woke me early. They were making such a racket outside the window. I was forced to get up and get dressed; the room was fairly nippy and damp. After breakfast, taking a ride with a truck driver, he drove on to Canterbury, in the county of Kent. The world famous Canterbury Cathedral became a shrine, after Archbishop Thomas Becket was murdered in the twelfth century. His devoted loyalty, to the Catholic Church, cost him his life at the hands of the knights of King Henry II. Later, this place of worship became the Mother Church for the Anglican Community. Exceptional wall decorations illuminated the halls. Few people in the middle-ages could read or write and the stained-glass window illustrations, educated the masses on stories from the Bible.

By the time we rolled into London, Europe's largest city, it was early evening. The night was still young so we continued to drift through this center of finance, banking and shipping. The wealth of cultural and political traditions were expressed in the fine old buildings, the famous museums and the numerous monuments. Meri pointed out Big Ben, the prominent bell in the clock tower of Westminster Abbey. Most English monarchs have been crowned, and many of them buried, in this Roman Catholic Cathedral, since the time of William the Conqueror. Passing by the House of Parliament, the country's supreme power monarch, members of the elite British government worked there, alongside the House of Lords, and the House of Commons. Melody groaned, she had seen enough of the ruling houses and was ready to do something more fun.

Trafalgar Square was named after the British naval victory over the French and Spanish fleets, off Cape Trafalgar Spain, during Napoleon's conquests. Coming across this unconventional plaza, it had been transformed into a flourishing hippie commune. Youthful flower girls, frolicked about in long full-skirts and see-through lace blouses. The braless women were covered with beaded vests and hand knitted scarves. Guys wore tight bell-bottom pants, flaunted by several cloth ties, and thick chains wrapped around their hips. Looking down at our plain shorts and unembellished sleeveless tops, we didn't quite fit in, with this flamboyant and flashy group of young people.

Heading on to Piccadilly Circus, the market place was full of antique stores and arts and crafts shops. Evidently, this spectacle was London's hub for meeting people. The statue of the Angel of Christian Charity, or "Eros," was a definite conversation piece. In almost every shop window were mannequins dressed in the latest "Mod" fashions. Plenty of skinny girls were hanging out in their "Twiggy" outfits. Temptations were everywhere; I just had to buy a jazzy little dress.

Stopping at a nearby restaurant, for lamb and lentils, we met a man who insisted on buying drinks at a local tavern. He introduced us to some of the band members at Lord Byron club on Carnaby and Beak Street. Conversations centered on the first anniversary of the Soviet invasion of Czechoslovakia. Some 50,000 demonstrators battled police with clubs and tanks at Wenceslas Square in Prague. Protesting had been going on for several days, and thousands were arrested during the violence. Sitting in silence, he spoke about a life that was hard for me to understand. The peaceful and prosperous existence, I lived in America, was the only life I had ever known.

Finishing our drinks, we set out to find a hotel for the night. With everything within walking distance, we took a stroll down Regent Street and Hyde Park. Walking was good exercise and it was helping me lose the weight I'd gained. Due to limited parking spaces in the big cities, the Europeans engaged in much more foot travel. Checking into a cheap hotel in the central part of town, after dropping off luggage, we headed for a discotheque. A full day ended with a last stop at "The Scotch of St. James" 13 Masons Yard, by Duke Street. We rejoined the night people!

Taking advantage of extra sleep time, the changing of the guards at Buckingham Palace didn't begin until late morning. Crowds of people turned out to watch the live soldiers, systematically switch places, after standing motionless for several hours. As hard as I tried to get one of the uniformed security to laugh, his stone face would not crack the slightest smile. The grand palace had been the London residence of Kings, and Queens, since the early eighteen-hundreds. Once owned by the Duke of Buckingham, this incredible home for the royal family has well over six-hundred rooms. Melody chided, she'd hate to be the maid in charge of cleaning-up their house. Hoping to get a glimpse of the Queen, me thinks she must have been out shopping for hats.

Leaving the palace, we headed toward St. James Park and down Oxford Street to see the Old Curiosity Shop. Charles Dickens, the popular English novelists of the Victorian era, once roamed these illustrious streets. After skipping breakfast, famished with hunger, we stopped for early lunch at an English Pub. The waiter suggested pie and mash, or minced-beef pie and mashed potatoes. Wolfing down the food, he offered black pudding for dessert. Seems this poor man's treat, has been around since the thirteenth century. I couldn't eat another bite, besides, it was too old.

Melody was broke and restricting activities was constantly on her mind. I should have given her some money but selfish thoughts consumed me. Not having much money myself, I was afraid to share what little I had. Shopping was a common weakness which ate up the funds we should have reserved for travel expenses. With only one week left before going back to the states, I was forced to cut back on any splurging. Money isn't everything but I needed to eat!

Hitchhiking in the cities was never easy and London was no exception. Two young English chaps pulled over, almost running up on to the sidewalk. Beckoning our way, they asked if we minded they make a stop by one of their homes in New Castle.

Going inside for hot tea and milk, we were at their mercy, as the interrogation began. Their British accents were harsh and heavy. Taking some time and effort to discern, I barely recognized the fast, paced, lingo. This interview, about our trip, was lengthy and hard to decipher, even though we spoke the same language.

Brian and Harry were eighteen year old kids and very inquisitive about how we managed to live in a foreign land. In the short time we talked, it became clear they were interested in travel and eager to learn from what we had to share. After finishing tea, and crumpets, the guys decided to drive to Scotland. They were hilarious, rushing around in a mad frenzy, grabbing food and things to take on the overnight escapade. Meri had an acquaintance staying in Edinburgh that summer. We were planning on spending the night with her. The guys said they could always sleep in their car, if necessary. I laughed at them the entire trip; they never shut-up. These high-strung youths had question after question, concerning every minor detail of our adventurous undertaking.

Driving into the capital of Scotland, in plain view, high on a crag, was the historic Edinburgh Castle. The dominate fortress towers are many feet above the town center. In this distinguished city, Princess Street divides the older historic sections and the newer region. Each segment has its own distinctive-character. According to my father, our family is of Scottish descent and I thought I might recognize a distant relative. I did see a face that looked very much like my younger brother Paul.

Meri called her friend, only to find out she was out of town for the week. With the art festival in progress, predictably, there were no vacancies. Catching the summer festivals in most towns we'd visited, the celebrations were entertaining but vacationing tourists filled most available rooms. We actually had better luck getting free rooms from strangers then we did with friends.

For the festivity in town, the men dressed in their native kilts in different sorts of plaid stoles and matching colored skirts. You could hear the traditional Highland music as bag pipes played and couples danced in the streets. As I listened to the melodies, fading away in the background, my thoughts drifted across the waters to the current situation and fighting between the Protestants and the Catholics in Northern Ireland. Would there ever be peace between the religions?

Having no luck finding a place to stay, and we weren't getting any offers from anyone off the street. Five beggars, instead of three, were probably not helping matters. Some nights were successes and some were failures, when it came to lodging destiny. Not always getting what we wanted, we were still responsible for alternative decisions to get what we needed. No one had any creative ideas for sleeping. Around midnight, the guys reluctantly suggested it might be best to drive home. Despondently climbing into their little red car, we headed back toward London.

About five in the morning, the car quit moving, we'd run out of gas. The night-time air was cool and no petrol station within sight. Pushing the car off to the side of the road, I tried waving down some help. Over an hour later, a sympathetic soul stopped to give a helping hand. The kind man shared a can of gasoline he had in the back of his truck. All summer long we'd been taking ride after ride and never once, did we offer to help pay for any gas. I was starting to have a guilt trip!

Just as the sun started to peek out, we drove up to the home of Brian Reed's brother and wife. Stopping unannounced, we woke the young couple and their three adorable little boys. The insane teen assured me his family wouldn't mind our unplanned intrusion. After utilizing the washroom, I returned to the parlor and sat down while the curious tots watched me in sleepy silence. Melody tried talking to them but they were too shy to speak to strangers. Brian's sister-in-law rustled up some chow, for everyone, as she listened to the guys ramble on and on about the whirlwind of a trip. Apologizing for our disturbance, she tried to reassure me it was not an imposition and she was happy to oblige.

Harry Douthwaite called his mother. I could tell from his exchange, she wasn't very happy with him keeping the car out over-night. Why was I not surprised he didn't get permission to go? As apologetic as we were, they kept saying over and over, it was the most memorable time they had ever experienced. They joked the U.K. would never be the same and they'd not have missed the fun for anything. Harry teased he was going to write a book and call it *Yankees Stay Home*. After wearing out our welcome, with this special family, the guys took us back to the motorway. Meri invited them both to Kansas City if they ever did make it over to the new world.

Although the overnight outing was exhilarating and exhausting, with those teenage British subjects, it was just another typical night for our trip. My traveling experience turned out to be everything and more than what I hoped it would be. Never, in my wildest imagination, could I have predicted the wacky encounters and outrageous adventures. My dream did come true!

This all encompassing travel lust had me hooked. Craving more, I knew I'd have to return someday to satisfy my endless hunger for traveling and immersing myself in other cultures. Something good happened everyday while on the road and I received much more than I gave. Not a summer's day went by that we didn't accept a free ride, a free meal, a free room or all three. The only way I could ever repay the numerous favors would be to do the same for others.

While waiting for the next pick-up and thinking about Brian and Harry, I trusted they would be able to travel to America one day and fulfill their dreams as well. Maybe I could help them in some small way, with a place to stay or a ride to a two-hundred year old historic landmark.

CHAPTER 10

—

SUNDAY, AUGUST 24

Taking a ride with a truck driver, we headed back through north central England. Climbing into transport trucks was never easy but we hardly ever turned down a ride. Driving through the county of Nottingham-shire along the River Trent, we proceeded on to Nottingham. Supposedly this town is where the legendary Robin Hood was born. This displaced, handsome nobleman robbed from the rich and gave to the poor. Eventually we drove past what remains of the original Sherwood Forest, where Robin allegedly lived with his band of outlaws. What was once an ancient royal hunting ground is protected by county parks, and has some of the oldest, and biggest, oak trees in the country. Those giant trees were certainly massive!

By the end of the day, the truck driver pulled up at a coed boarding house in the township of Leicester. Most of the guests were men, in this truck-stop for drivers with big-rigs. Meri and I rented a single room and slipped Melody in afterward. She elected to stay in and not go out for food, fearing someone would catch our deceitfulness. We couldn't persuade her at this point.

Meri and I ventured out for something to eat and to find a church for Sunday evening Mass. Kneeling in adoration, I thanked God again for my many blessings and good fortune. Believing in the power of prayer, we still had a few days on the road and needed continued safe direction.

Leaving church, I could hear the sounds of rock music coming from a near-by park pavilion. Stopping to listen to the pop concert, we watched the young people in their bright freaky outfits. Everyone was sitting on the grass and doing whatever made them feel good: making out, smoking pot, singing, or just dancing to the tunes. In the crowd of kids was one of the school boys we met while working at the hotel in Interlaken. After a short visit, we bid him goodnight and walked back to the boarding-house. Melody was writing letters home as we shared our fruit and cheese with her.

Breakfast was included in the nights lodging so we got to eat more than the usual hard rolls. Consuming until our stomachs could hold no more, one of the trucker boarders offered a ride. He was going to the old countryside of Oxford-shire, along the River Thames and was happy to have passengers. The talkative burley driver, Barry Rodgers from Yorkshire, was an amateur boxer. His chatter centered on Joe Frazier defeating Jerry Quarry in the heavy weight title bout at the Madison Square Garden in New York. Boxing was not a sport I followed and I had absolutely no idea who he was talking about. Melody rolled her eyes while nodding her head, as if she was remotely interested. Passing by a time-honored college campus, Barry said the University of Oxford was the best in Great Britain. This outstanding school began classes in the twelfth century.

Driving through England was certainly a history lesson in motion. The presence of the past was almost overpowering. Meri followed the map in the guide book, pointing to the various historic places as we passed them and briefing me on the different county seats. It helped to have a knowledgeable driver who knew about the old landmark buildings. Barry continued on through Warwickshire, along the River Avon, pointing to an old medieval castle. Could it be Camelot?

Bouncing along in the truck, four adults riding in the front seat, Barry mentioned the important birthplace of William Shakespeare, in Stratford-upon-Avon. Wishing I knew more about the poet and dramatist, he wrote some of the greatest plays, comedies, tragedies, and romances ever written. The Merchant of Venice, Romeo and Juliet, Anthony and Cleopatra, were but a few brought to mind. Meri wanted to stop and see the house where Will was born. With Barry's help, we slithered down from the truck cab, wishing he had a ladder. Listening to the sounds of the grinding truck gears, shifting loudly, we waived to Mr. Rodgers as he drove on down the road.

Taking a short tour of the historic birth house, we learned William was only fifty-two years old when he died. As we left the county of Warwick, an animated Scotsman offered a ride on into London. Driving past the fourteenth-century Holy Trinity Church, where Shakespeare was baptized and later buried, last but not least, the final well known attraction was the majestic Windsor Castle. This English regal residence still looks like a medieval fortress with towers and terraces housing the State apartments. The palace continues to be the oldest, and largest, occupied castle in the entire world.

We were dropped off in London right at dusk. Fortunately, we accepted another ride with a man who was driving the entire way to Dover. Arriving close to midnight, in the dense fog, our ride treated three starving girls to fish and chips enclosed in brown paper wrappings. The English chips are very similar to what Americans call French fries and the fish were deep-fried in a heavy batter coating. Not eating anything since breakfast, I ate every crumb of the crispy fritters. They were great!

Across the street from the fast food restaurant was the YMCA. Walking over to get a room, the doors were tightly locked. I kept ring, ring, ringing the bell until someone came to the entrance. Closed because of a full house, the keeper said we could stay in the reading room, if we didn't mind sleeping on the floor. Was he kidding? We were the queens of makeshift lodging. Too tired and cold to look for another place, we were happy to take his offer. Handing out blankets and pillows, he pointed to the washroom and said there'd be no charge for the floor. How sweet those words sounded to our penniless ears. My worn-out body fell fast asleep on the hardwood bed.

Daybreak rolled around quickly since we had to get to the docks early to catch the free ferry. A familiar crewman waved as we boarded without tickets. One of the men ushered his stowaways to the control room where we observed the instruments and machinery manning the ship. The seaport, of the Straits of Dover, was in clear view as we drifted away from the shore. The massive white cliffs, surrounding the narrowest part of the Channel, faced towards Continental Europe. This nearest point to France, from Great Britain, was originally fortified by the Romans.

While crossing the North Sea, Melody met a couple of guys on the ferryboat who were headed to Spain. Reassured, I was glad to know she wouldn't have to travel alone. Dreading this moment, it was time for the three of us to separate. Mel had made up her mind. She would go back to Spain to find her relatives. Envious of her determination to stay longer, I questioned whether going back to college was in my best interest. Reminding myself of other obligations, I had to think more responsibly.

Folding my arms around Melody, we both started to cry. Apologizing for not helping her out more, I worried she would never forgive me for being so greedy. She reminded me there would be money waiting in Spain and she could get her stored items after she was settled. This good-bye was by far, one the toughest I had to make. Meri had tears in her eyes as we both watched Melody and the guys drive away. Wiping away the tears trying to be strong, we had to move on.

Meri and I headed on to Brussels Belgium, taking a ride from a young man by the name of Percy Salembier. The rain was coming down so hard that it was difficult to see the fatal car accident ahead. Percy knew of a youth hostel in the central part of town where he let us off. Several female students from the U.S. were staying in the gloomy basement dorm rooms. Everyone shared stories of vacation travels and work experiences. However, Meri and I were the only females with stories of hitchhiking. The other girls were astounded at our common mode of transportation. Me too!

The dismal day fit my reflexive mood as I sat thinking about how fast the summer had flown by. Although I missed my family and friends, there were still tons of places and other countries calling my name. Sleep came quickly after several nights of interrupted rest.

As much as I would have liked to lie around the next morning, we wanted to get out and see some of the city's highlights. Brussels, another large city, had numerous exceptional buildings and monuments. The capital of Belgium is the headquarters of NATO, the North Atlantic Treaty Organization, as well as the European Union. Walking past the Royal Palace, with offices of the King, we ventured into Art Nouveau, a museum featuring both ancient and modern Flemish Art. Hurrying through another thirteenth-century cathedral, we had to do last minute souvenir shopping in the flea market. Last but not least, we watched the Brussels water boy, "Mannken Pis." This small fountain statue is the cute little naked baby going potty into a tiny pool. He certainly brought giggles from onlookers.

Back at the hostel, we were invited out for dinner with some of the other American girls. In their rented car, we cruised around the town squares and up and down the crowded boulevards. Circling the Grand Sablon, which divides Lower Town and Upper Town, we saw the majestic fifteenth century, Hotel de Ville. This attractive Gothic building was covered with dozens of arched windows and many fine sculptures. People everywhere were talking, eating, and promenading through the parks. Gazing out the car window, I let my melancholy mood get the best of me. Trying to change my miserable state of mind, I switched my thoughts to Melody, hoping she was getting along okay.

While chatting with the girls, it didn't take long to surmise they came from affluent families. Briefly bothered by the fact I didn't have unlimited funds for travel, my mind started churning. There had to be a way I could come up with the resources to continue my passion. Sitting there thinking about options, I could finish another year of school and become an airline stewardess.

Travel privileges through a flight career would be one way to solve my quandary. It was amazing how much better I felt once I decided how to return the following year and pick up where I left off. Meri was the first to hear of the unlimited travel possibilities, as I informed her of my plan.

Rain showers were unrelenting the next morning. No wonder I was down in the dumps! It was raining when we first arrived in Europe and our last days were ending in a wash. Recalling the more sunny days, how could I forget those very hot days on the Riviera. Out on the street, a young boy by the name of Andre Fraiture took us to the highway. Right away, a robust German man in a white Mercedes furnished a ride to Luxembourg. Although it was out of his way, Jean Schaus elected to do this favor for two lovely American girls. Before the train station drop-off, he was kind enough to buy our lunch and glasses of port wine. Gathering up our stored luggage and boxes, we walked across the street to get a room for the last night. Where did the summer go?

Holding on tight to my bags, we rented a room in the same hotel where my suitcase was lifted. After checking in, Meri and I took a leisurely walk around the town. Not so long ago, this country was a strange and alien place. In only three short months, we'd grown familiar and accustomed to the habits of these foreign lands. Living and working in two different countries, we toured a dozen more and met countless people from all over the world. Life would never be the same!

The places, experiences, and lessons learned, would change my life forever. Alive and well, I could actually feel a difference in my character. No longer the person that arrived the first day of summer, the growth was positive. I was more confident, more self-assured, and more mature. I'm sure I was wiser to the ways of the world but had not lost my self-respect. Despite a small number of misfortunes, which only added more excitement to the trip, the time was well spent.

After some very compact packing, we went out to eat with a couple of guys we met in the lobby. Rick Clark, and his friend Ralph, were headed home from Germany after learning the language. Needless to say, I didn't become fluent in German but I could speak more than when I first arrived. Meri became more proficient in her French skills. Running into other students from the states, it was that time of year, everyone heading back to school after spending time abroad. I noticed less self-absorption and a little more self-awareness in the stimulating conversations.

Some of the students had a gathering in their room to listen to some of the latest music tunes. Most everyone was smoking pot but I wasn't interested. Enjoying my time away so much, I didn't want to escape, not even temporarily. My gratifications in life were derived from the realities of life. I hadn't suffered enough pain in my twenty plus years to have to medicate any hurts or injuries. Someone, in the jam-packed room, announced the birth of a new baby girl to Paul and Linda McCartney. New life was certainly something to celebrate as I smiled at the happy news.

Sleeping late the next morning, our flight didn't leave until later in the afternoon. Eating my last hard roll and bitter coffee, for now, there were definitely a few things I was looking forward to back home. Eggs and toast for breakfast again would be wonderful. If it hadn't been for the orange marmalade jam, I'm not sure I could have eaten the tough white bread. My mouth watered just thinking about a thick, juicy Angus beef steak. Europeans were not into T-bones like most of the well-fed, chunky Americans. Their food portions were smaller and you didn't see many overweight people in Europe. My clothes weren't fitting snug anymore. I'd lost those extra pounds.

Having lots of time to get ready, Meri and I decided to dress-up for the plane ride to America. The dress I wore was regal blue with a white French-lace overlay. Buying it on sale, at a cut-rate store in London, it only looked expensive. Justifying the purchase, Meri and Melody would take back their clothes I borrowed, and of course, I would have to have something to wear.

Before heading to the airport, we stopped by the embassy. Checking one last time, I wanted to see if there was any word about my stolen suitcase. Some lucky girl in Luxembourg was wearing my brand-new outfit. Inspecting some of the people on the sidewalk, I thought I might see a lady walking down the street in my red-and-white-striped dress. As we exited the door of the embassy, another guy entered behind me. He had just arrived from the states to begin his European quest.

Back at the hotel, we loaded bags and belongings in the rented car of the guys we met the night before. Heading out of town, in a misty rain, we stopped to pick up some wine, bread, and cheese. Eating in the car, before check-in, everyone offered travel tips and information learned about the different countries where we'd worked and spent time. We were the experts now!

Inspired by another thought, maybe someday I could be a tour guide and take groups to other countries. I would have to become fluent in several languages (like the Italians) and take more history classes. Going on into the airport terminal, we ran into the kids we'd partied with the night before. Wishing them safe journeys, everyone headed off to their respective concourses.

The Icelandic airplane was having mechanical difficulties and all the passengers were rebooked on an Air-France Flight. After a short stopover in Paris, in the early evening hours of August the twenty-ninth, the jumbo jet took off for the eight hour transatlantic trip back over the ocean.

Flying home was much faster but no less bumpy. In fact, the male steward accidentally knocked over a glass of orange-juice on my brand-new dress. He was mortified and I was saturated by the sticky mess. After patting myself with a dry cloth, I ended up going to the rest-room and rinsing out my clothing in the sink. Placing the water-soaked outfit into a plastic bag, I wore my knee-length raincoat back to my seat. Oh, well! I didn't really need to wear a dress all night anyway. My spanking-new garment was a dry-clean-only material. It would never be the same again!

The remainder of the flight could not have been more first rate. The flight attendant passed out carte du jour for dinners: ham from Bayonne, breast of duckling with burgundy wine sauce, green peas, Paysanne cheese, pastry, Café De Colombie and French red wine or champagne. Taking a couple of hours to serve the food, we spent several more hours eating and drinking. After a few bubbly drinks, I completely forgot about sitting with nothing but my underwear on.

Awake the remainder of the night, I talked, laughed, and reminisced with Meri about our most fantastic summer. It would be hard to return to life as I knew it before. There was a bigger world out there! My attitude toward school was changing. Education was not only found in a classroom. Would I be able to express myself in ways that used to be hard for me? Europeans were superior in articulating their thoughts and expressing their feelings. Learning to think outside myself, I would try not to be so judgmental, complain less and enjoy life more. We survived a miraculous trip!

Closing my blurry eyes for a while, I thanked God for the abundance of gifts He'd given me the summer of '69. I must have dozed off for a short time, because the next thing I knew, we were preparing to land. The journey was over! Back in the U.S.A., we landed safely in New York.

After getting off the plane, there was talk in the airport about a hijacked TWA flight over Italy. The plane was seized, by two Arab commandos, while flying from Los Angeles to Tel Aviv. They were objecting to the sale of American fighter jets to Israel. For the time being, I was glad to be back on U.S. soil. Proceeding on, I gathered up my possessions to go through customs.

Calling the Burkes again, we'd planned to spend another night with them before flying back to Missouri. Such a short time had passed since we were last there and yet so much had transpired. We were anxious to tell everyone about the traveling, the work, and the many countries we'd visited. The awesome and humbling report included only a couple of our wild and crazy stories.

The following day we took another plane to Chicago and eventually ended up in Kansas City. Sitting next to me on this flight was a guy by the name of Josh Stein from Evanston, Illinois. He worked in New York City while going to school and was headed home for Labor Day weekend. I encouraged him to take advantage of the student work-exchange program through his college. I wanted to tell the whole world about my summer adventure. Josh probably thought I was nutty!

Landing without incident, the first thing I did was make a collect call home to inform my parents I was back in the Show

Me State. It was good to hear their voices again after three long months. Meri's older brother, Butch, met us at the airport. Driving on to Springfield in his convertible, he made sure we made it back in time for class registration at Southwest Missouri State.

Driving up the long winding driveway, Larry and Robert, the youngest of my five brothers, were waiting outside next to the white-picket fence. Giving everyone a big hug, I couldn't thank my parents enough for allowing me the incredible opportunity to work, and play, in Europe. I learned more in those three short months then in my three previous years of formal schooling.

There was a letter waiting from Melody. She did have trouble getting to her destination, but she was out of danger and enjoying her time in Moguer Spain. Apparently, she left her passport in the car she rode off from the ferry. Consequently, with no credentials or proof of identity, she was forced to spend a night in a police station. Poor girl! The guys were thoughtful enough to send her passport on to her cousins. Sometimes a crisis makes the best story. She made it safely. Bravo!

A few more letters beat me home. Claudio was still working in Frankfurt, his English had much improved and his marriage proposal was still good. Chris and Bruno finished out their summer contract in Germany and were back in Rome. They were preparing to report for military duty. Lenny would head to Rye, New York, by the end of the year and was looking forward to a reunion. He promised to send my box of possessions as soon as possible. Carmelo was working in Horben, Switzerland, and Raffaele returned to Sassari in Sardinia, Italy. Wladimiro, with few words, sent his love and concern. Even Brian and Harry wrote, checking to see if we made it back in one piece. They were looking forward to visiting our young country and seeing the land of milk and honey. Assuming our meeting was an inspiration, I fully expected to see them within the year.

On Sunday, August thirty-first, the great adventure ended. Feeling the jet lag as well as some emotional letdown, my energy level was fading. In the comfort of my rural country home, I could relax and pass out the gifts I carried half-way around the world. Every item had a story, where it came from and how it was acquired. Sharing most of those stories with my parents and brothers, after a few hours, everyone grew weary of my tales. Life at home returned to usual household tasks and daily routines. Pensively putting away my things, I started thinking about tomorrow.

Summers are about having fun and this trip was the greatest summer of my life. Besides the wealth of knowledge and information gained, over my break from academia, I grew up very fast. Experience is by far the best teacher. I would never again let the unexpected get in the way of my seeking out new places and making new acquaintances. Surprises make the most wonderful, and lasting memories, especially if they're shared with zealous friends. Life is a winding road!

Girlfriends, I can never say enough about the value of having girlfriends. Priceless allies in times of need, they are never far away and sometimes they even break the rules with you. They can be the best travel companions for good times and great conversation. Time and miles may come between you, but they are always close at hand. The world would not be the same without women friends to cheer you on, share your joys, and comfort your sorrows. Women need each other, more than ever as we get older. Thank you my many girlfriends, and especially, Meri and Melody.

ABOUT THE AUTHOR

This is my first attempt at writing, other than college papers and work-related reports. My formal educational background is in social work, and secondary guidance and counseling. After spending twenty years working in the medical field, I was employed part time at a mountain resort and sold real estate in the state of Washington before returning to Missouri in spring 2009.

One of my long-term goals was to write a book about my summer in 1969, when I worked and traveled in Western Europe with two girlfriends. Traveling extensively since that summer, I have never had another trip come anywhere close to the extreme adventure. I wanted to share the great escapade with others who love to travel, and especially with those who grew up in the sixties. This story can be enjoyed by the young and the old who love having fun while traveling and visiting other countries.

Growing up in the Midwest, I was the only girl in a large Catholic family with five brothers. My mom tried to keep me feminine in dresses, dance, and piano lessons. I tried to keep up with the boys, riding horses and climbing trees on our rural southern Missouri acreage. Higher learning and travel were valued by my father. He encouraged me to do both as time and funds allowed.

As a child, I spent my summers boating and water skiing in warm-water lakes. During several years of my adult life, I traveled and lived in the beautiful state of Colorado. I took advantage of competitive running, snow skiing, hiking, and biking while in the great Rocky Mountains.

Considering myself privileged, I have had a wonderful time living in the States and abroad. Although my life has not always been easy, it has been good. My three grown children and four beautiful grandchildren are special gifts as well as my new husband. My Extended family and numerous friends are an important part of my life. I am blessed!

CPSIA information can be obtained at www.ICGtesting.com
Printed in the USA
LVOW040747231211

260742LV00001B/409/P